D1564781

SMART MONEY

FOR THE BACKSIDE OF LIFE

SAVVY STRATEGIES FOR A REWARDING RETIREMENT

BRIAN MIRAU

Copyright © 2022 by Brian Mirau.

All rights reserved. No part of this publication may be reproduced, distributed, or transmitted in any form or by any means, including photocopying, recording, or other electronic or mechanical methods, without the prior written permission of the publisher, except in the case of brief quotations embodied in critical reviews and certain other noncommercial uses permitted by copyright law. For permission requests, write to the publisher at the address below. These materials are provided to you by Brian Mirau for informational purposes only and Brian Mirau and Advisors Excel, LLC expressly disclaim any and all liability arising out of or relating to your use of same. The provision of these materials does not constitute legal or investment advice and does not establish an attorney-client relationship between you and Brian Mirau. No tax advice is contained in these materials. You are solely responsible for ensuring the accuracy and completeness of all materials as well as the compliance, validity, and enforceability of all materials under any applicable law. The strategies found within may not be suitable for every situation. You are expressly advised to consult with a qualified attorney or other professional in making any such determination and to determine your legal or financial needs. No warranty of any kind, implied, expressed, or statutory, including but not limited to the warranties of title and non-infringement of third-party rights, is given with respect to this publication.

Brian Mirau/Mirau Capital Management, Inc.
1860 Sudderth Drive
Ruidoso, NM 88345

Book layout ©2022 Advisors Excel, LLC

Smart Money for the Backside of Life. — 1st edition.

ISBN 9798849441603

Brian Mirau is registered as an Investment Advisor Representative and is a licensed insurance agent in the states of NM, TX, CO, and IL. Mirau Capital Management is an independent financial services firm that helps individuals create retirement strategies using a variety of investment and insurance products to custom suit their needs and objectives.

Securities and advisory services offered through Madison Avenue Securities, LLC ("MAS"), a registered investment advisor. Member FINRA and SIPC. Mirau Capital Management, Inc. and MAS are not affiliated entities. Licensed to do business in the following states: NM, TX, CO, FL, GA, KY, MN, NC, NV, OK, TN, and UT.

The contents of this book are provided for informational purposes only and are not intended to serve as the basis for any financial decisions. Any tax, legal, or estate planning information is general in nature. It should not be construed as legal or tax advice. Always consult an attorney or tax professional regarding the applicability of this information to your unique situation.

Information presented is believed to be factual and up-to-date, but we do not guarantee its accuracy, and it should not be regarded as a complete analysis of the subjects discussed. All expressions of opinion are those of the author as of the date of publication and are subject to change. Content should not be construed as personalized investment advice nor should it be interpreted as an offer to buy or sell any securities mentioned. A financial advisor should be consulted before implementing any of the strategies presented.

Investing involves risk, including the potential loss of principal. No investment strategy can guarantee a profit or protect against loss in periods of declining values. Any references to protection benefits or guaranteed/lifetime income streams refer only to fixed insurance products, not securities or investment products. Insurance and annuity product guarantees are backed by the financial strength and claims-paying ability of the issuing insurance company.

The Forbes rankings of America's Top Financial Security Professionals, developed by SHOOK Research, is based on an algorithm of qualitative criterion. This is an unpaid acknowledgment. Forbes, SHOOK Research, and MAS are unaffiliated entities. Any media logos and/or trademarks contained herein are the property of their respective owners and no endorsement by those owners of our firm is stated or implied.

Any names used in the examples in this book are hypothetical only and do not represent actual clients.

Table of Contents

The Importance of Planning

W e have all heard the old adage that an ounce of prevention is worth a pound of cure. I have had the privilege of visiting with many individuals and couples through the years and discussing with them the importance of having a complete game plan in place for the next phase of life called RETIREMENT.

After having the privilege of being a student-athlete who played football in high school and college, I learned a significant lesson. All elements of the game—offense, defense, kicking game, and special teams demand team unity and most of all, a great coach who has prepared and coordinated a well-constructed game plan. The plan must be flexible but also contain fundamental elements in order to have success at the end of a game.

This preparation did not happen in pregame warmups. Rather, it began the previous spring by spending the necessary time working in the weight room, executing drills, building speed and endurance, and most of all, uniting with teammates to discover strengths and weaknesses. We can have the best athletes, the best coaches, the best equipment, and the best stadiums but if we do not understand how to work together and support each other as a team, while committing to the discipline necessary to engage in preparation, it would be very difficult to attain success.

I have found that planning for the back side of life—retirement—is not any different. We can save, save, save for the older person we will someday become, but if we are not paying attention to the details in the process, we can find ourselves totally missing the mark. There must be a coordinated effort in the planning process to examine details such as taxes, inflation, investment risk, fees, longevity, legal planning, and coaching. We must always plan for the worst and hope for the best. It is better to plan for life events and not need to implement certain contingencies than to be struck with a life event and not be prepared to deal with it. In life, I believe we deal with two kinds of pain, the pain involved with preparation and discipline, or the pain of regret for not being prepared to deal with a life-altering event.

We all have a choice. I have found that through all my years of athletics and professional development, there has been one common denominator that generated my opportunities for success—a great coach. A great coach has pointed me in the right direction when I have fallen astray. A great coach has brought me encouragement when I got weary and worn down. A great coach has taught me the basics over and over when I chose to out-smart myself.

The planning for the backside of life is much different today than it was for previous generations. In the past, many people worked hard, had company pensions, and tried to save regularly to plan for the older person they would someday become. In today's world, as a whole, people are living longer and need to plan to make sure that their lifestyle income lasts longer than they do. In today's world, we don't see as many pensions that provide a guaranteed lifetime income. This really puts the pressure on the retirees today to make sure that their money lasts longer than they do. Many things are pulling at our dollars today—taxes, inflation, health care costs, unnecessary fees and expenses, costs related to helping our children, costs related to helping our parents, long-term care expenses . . . the list goes on and on.

I find that after working with hundreds of folks tons of landmines pop up and require preparation. You can find yourself in a bad way. I believe that it is important to understand this journey and three phases of retirement you will encounter. I believe we must not fall prey to some of the myths about retirement that I so commonly hear.

The primary myth I hear too often:

"We won't need as much income in retirement as we did in our working years." Most folks don't want to reduce their standard of living the day they retire. In fact, most enter into the first phase of retirement called the go-go phase. They plan on doing the things that they were unable to do because of being bound to employment, such as travel, RVing, home projects, time with children and grandchildren, more time with spouses, golfing, hiking, working out, volunteering, and many other various hobbies, events, and activities. Again, the list goes on and on and most of these opportunities take money. I believe it's important to visualize your retirement dreams and put together the necessary game plan to make sure it happens. You have the power to make sure it happens if you take the right steps, visualize and dream, prepare, get the necessary coaching, and take action that helps you gain control.

Growing up, I did not have a lot of material belongings, but I had what I needed. I was taught and have learned through the years the values and principles of commitment, honesty, discipline, hard work, the importance of finishing the task at hand, the importance of being on time, the value of a relationship with Jesus Christ my Father, the importance of continual study, the value of mistakes, the opportunity to learn and grow from these mistakes, and the value of family (parents, grandparents, my AMAZING wife, children, and now grandchildren).

I have learned to value so many things, large and small. My list, much like yours I'm sure, is quite extensive:

Preparation
A journey
Watching my wife give birth to our children
Teaching others
Generosity
Forgiveness

Humility

Tenderness

Love

Doing what you say you will do

Having peace in my life

Having boundaries

Having good friends

Having a good dog

A great workout

Good barbecue, or just about any food

An incredible sunrise or sunset

Playing catch with any ball

Hugging my children

Prayer

Making it to the top of the mountain

The smell of a campfire

A good cup of coffee

Traveling to watch the kids play anything

A walk with my wife

Having money in our pockets

Catching a fish alongside my dad

Being exhausted and weary

Working on my own truck or car

Entrepreneurship

My grandmother teaching me how to make a chocolate cake
with coffee

Building a team

Accountability

My mother lifting me up after a tough challenge

Teaching and coaching children

Praying for others

Saying I'm sorry

Experiencing success

Watching my children both succeed and fail

Taking risks

Good music

Planting something and watching it grow

Hearing a bull elk screaming early in the morning

A hard-fought win

Seeing wild horses

Feeding the masses good food

Finally, the most incredible value is that of having amazing mentors and coaches in my life to reach out and coach me through my journey. The top of that list begins with Jesus Christ my Lord.

I have made way too many mistakes over my life to begin mentioning any of them, but I have learned to become dependent on all of my life coaches and mentors. I have been truly blessed through the wisdom they shared with me throughout my lifetime.

This is why I wanted to take time to share just a few thoughts and ideas on the financial aspects that many of us deal with to ensure that we can plan and expect the most out of this season we refer to as the "Backside of Life."

Potential Risks to Your Ideal Retirement

Ever feel like life gets in the way and prevents you from doing things you should not ignore? I think if we're honest with ourselves, we've all put off obligations we know are important.

In your case, you may be reading this book because it's time to get serious about financial planning and, specifically, devising a way to best prepare for retirement. A retirement income plan should be based on more components than just your investments or your finances. The preparation of that strategy begins with your desires, ambitions, and goals for this fulfilling season of life.

There's no such thing as a silly question. Not when one of the most common questions we hear from folks regarding retirement is, "Am I going to be okay?" Often, it seems, people are reluctant to meet with financial professionals because they worry they might sound uneducated. Yet, it's understandable for you to be a novice when it comes to financial issues and retirement concerns. You've been busy with your lives and your careers. Time spent away from work has meant time spent being around those you love and engaging in the activities you enjoy. Retirement provides the opportunity to do even more of that, while not fretting over work obligations.

Concerns people have about what they may encounter during retirement can be far-reaching and still perfectly legitimate. For a quick snapshot, I want to provide a brief sampling of wide-ranging issues that can come up during discussions about what to potentially brace for in retirement. This book will touch on many of these issues in further detail.

Politics: A presidential election often stirs emotions regarding potential effects on the economy. Investors grow anxious about how a new president can influence market returns. It's Congress, however, that establishes tax laws and passes spending bills. Yet the president can indirectly affect the economy and the stock market in various ways such as the appointment of policymakers, development of international relations, and influential sway on new legislation.

Taxes: An example of a president's influence can be cited in signature legislation passed during Donald Trump's presidency, the Tax Cuts and Jobs Act of 2017. However, our tax system remains progressive, so the more you earn, the higher the tax rate within each tax bracket of subsequently higher income. A thorough understanding of tax regulations can be crucial. A financial professional can help identify potential issues a tax professional can help solve.

Inflation: Government spending, which most recently spiked with relief packages designed to assist U.S. citizens during the COVID-19 pandemic, can fuel concerns of inflationary hikes stemming from an influx of money thrust at the same consumer goods. A retiree's income can be impacted by the effect inflation can have on a fixed budget. The value of currency decreases because inflation erodes purchasing power.

Health pandemic: The coronavirus outbreak could impact how Americans view risks and re-examine healthy habits. That, potentially, could be one of the effects of COVID-19 as we assess how long a pandemic can last and if others will occur in our lifetimes. The cost of health care can be surprising throughout retirement. It could become an issue people focus on even more following the pandemic, which had a particularly acute impact on some U.S. elder care facilities.

Cybersecurity: Think you'll give up your smartphone in retirement? No way, right? It's here to stay, along with other intellectual gadgetry, including devices that have not been patented or invented. Retirees are becoming more tech-savvy, yet they can also be more trusting, which can be problematic when responding to potential scammers by phone, text, or email. Cybercrime often uses technology to target potential victims. Scammers, much like technology, figure to only grow more sophisticated over time.

CHAPTER 1

Longevity

You would think the prospect of the grave would loom more frightening as we age, yet many retirees say their number one concern is actually running out of money in their twilight years.[1] This fear is, unfortunately, justified, in part, because of one significant factor: We're living longer.

According to the Social Security Administration, in 1950, the average life expectancy for a sixty-five-year-old man was seventy-eight, and the average for a sixty-five-year-old woman was eighty-one. In 2021, those averages were 83 and 86.8, respectively.[2]

The bottom line of many retirees' budget woes comes down to this: They just didn't plan to live so long. Now, when we are younger and in our working years, that's not something we necessarily see as a bad thing; don't some people fantasize about living forever or, at least, reaching the ripe old age of one hundred?

However, with a longer lifespan, as we near retirement, we face a few snags. Our resources are finite—we only have so much money to provide income—but our lifespans can be

---

[1] Liz Weston. nerdwallet.com. March 25, 2021. "Will You Really Run Out of Money in Retirement?"
https://www.nerdwallet.com/article/finance/will-you-really-run-out-of-money-in-retirement
[2] Social Security Administration. 2011 Trustees Report. "Actuarial Publications: Cohort Life Expectancy."
https://www.ssa.gov/OACT/TR/2011/lr5a4.html

unpredictably long, perhaps longer than our resources allow. Also, longer lives don't necessarily equate with healthier lives. The longer you live, the more money you will likely need to spend on health care, even excluding long-term care needs like nursing homes.

You will also run into inflation. If you don't plan to live another twenty-five years but end up doing so, inflation at an average 3 percent will approximately double the price of goods over that time period. Put a harsh twist on that and the buying power of a ninety-year-old will be half of what they possessed if they retired at sixty-five.[3] And this is before you count the expenses of any potential health care or long-term care needs.

Because we don't necessarily get to have our cake and eat it, too, our collective increased longevity hasn't necessarily increased the healthy years of our lives. Typically, our life-extending care most widely applies to the time in our lives where we will need more care in general. Think of common situations like a pacemaker at eighty-five, or cancer treatment at seventy-eight.

"Wow, Brian," I can hear you say. "Way to start with the good news first."

I know, I've painted a grim picture, but all I'm concerned about here is cost. It's hard to put a dollar sign on life, but that is essentially what we're talking about when discussing longevity and finances. Living longer isn't a bad thing; it just costs more, and one key to a sound retirement strategy is preparing for it in advance.

One woman I know of illustrates this picture perfectly.

Her mother passed away in her late seventies after years of suffering from Alzheimer's disease. Her father died at eighty from cancer. With modern medicine and treatment, this woman survived two rounds of breast cancer, lived with diabetes, and endured a pacemaker, extending her life to age

---

3 Bob Sullivan, Benjamin Curry. Forbes. April 28, 2021. "Inflation And Retirement Investments: What You Need to Know."
https://www.forbes.com/advisor/retirement/inflation-retirement-investments/

eighty-eight, nearly a decade beyond what she anticipated. However, she and her husband had saved and planned for "just in case," trying to be prepared just in case they had to move, just in case they needed nursing home care, and just in case they needed to help children and grandchildren with their expenses.

One of their "just-in-case" scenarios addressed living much longer than they anticipated. The last six years of her life were fraught with medical expenses, but she was also blessed with knowing her five great-grandchildren and building everlasting relationships with her children and grandchildren. She was able to pay for her own medical care, including her final two years in a nursing home, and her twilight years were truly golden. From age eighty-five to eighty-eight, she was more socially active, with many visits from family and friends, and she participated in more activities than she had in the seven years since her husband died.

When she passed away, her planning from decades earlier allowed her to pass on a legacy to her children. In some ways that can be calculated in dollar signs *and* in ways that can't. Living longer may be more expensive, but it can be so meaningful when you plan for what-ifs and just-in-cases.

Example: One woman I know illustrates this picture perfectly. Her mother passed away in her late seventies after years of suffering from Alzheimer's disease. Her father died at eighty from cancer. With modern medicine and treatment, this woman survived two rounds of breast cancer, lived with diabetes, and relied on a pacemaker, extending her life to age eighty-eight, nearly a decade beyond what she anticipated. However, she and her husband had saved and planned for "just in case," trying to be prepared if they had to move, needed nursing home care, or needed to help children and grandchildren with their expenses. One of their "just-in-case" scenarios was living much longer than they anticipated. The last six years of her life were fraught with medical expenses, but she was also blessed with knowing her five great-grandchildren and deepening relationships with her children and grandchildren. She was able to pay for her own medical care, including her final two years in a nursing home, and her twilight years were truly golden.

From age eighty-five to eighty-eight, she was more socially active, with many visits from family and friends. She participated in more activities than she had in the seven years since her husband died. Her planning from decades earlier allowed her to pass on a legacy to her children when she passed away herself. The legacy she left behind can be measured both in dollar signs *and* in other intangible ways.

Living longer may be more expensive, but it can be so meaningful when you plan for your "just-in-cases."

Retiring Early

A key part of planning for retirement revolves around retirement income. After all, retirement is cutting the cord that tethers you to your employer—and your monthly check. However, that check often comes with many other benefits, particularly health care. Health care is often the thing that can unexpectedly put dreams for an early retirement on hold. Some employers offer health benefits to their retired workers, but that number has declined drastically over the past several decades. In 1988, among employers who offered health benefits to their workers, 66 percent offered health benefits to their retirees. That number has since diminished to 29 percent.[4]

So, with employer-offered retirement health benefits on the wane, this becomes a major point of concern for anyone who is looking to retire, particularly those who are looking to retire before age sixty-five, when they would become eligible for Medicare coverage. Fidelity estimates that the average retired couple at age sixty-five will need approximately $300,000 for

---

4 Henry J. Kaiser Family Foundation. October 8, 2020. "2020 Employer Health Benefits Survey Section Eleven: Retiree Health Benefits." https://www.kff.org/report-section/ehbs-2020-section-11-retiree-health-benefits/

medical expenses, not including long-term care.[5] Do you think it's likely that cost will decrease?

Even if you are working until age sixty-five or have plans to cover your health expenses until that point, I often have clients who incorrectly assume Medicare is their golden ticket to cover all expenses. That is simply not the case.

Retiring Later

Planning for a long life in retirement partly depends on when you retire. While many people end up retiring earlier than they anticipated—due to injuries, layoffs, family crises, and other unforeseen circumstances—continuing to work past age sixty (and even sixty-five) is still a viable option for others and can be an excellent way to help establish financial comfort in retirement.

There are many reasons for this. For one, you obviously still earn a paycheck and the benefits accompanying it. Medical coverage and beefing up your retirement accounts with further savings can be significant by themselves but continuing your income also should keep you from dipping into your retirement funds, further allowing them the opportunity to grow.

Additionally, for many workers, their nine-to-five job is more than just clocking in and out. Having a sense of purpose can keep us active physically, mentally, and socially. That kind of activity and level of engagement may also help stave off many of the health problems that plague retirees. Avoiding a sedentary life is one of the advantages of staying plugged into the workforce, if possible.

For many of our retired clients who are thriving in retirement, I hear all the time, "We're busier now than we ever were in our working years." This is because they have chosen to not retire from their lives just because they retired from their

---

5 Fidelity Viewpoints. Fidelity. May 6, 2021. "How to Plan for Rising Health Care Costs." https://www.fidelity.com/viewpoints/personal-finance/plan-for-rising-health-care-costs

jobs. I see more and more of our clients very active in their churches, schools, local charities, and holding down various part-time jobs around town. Even though most have done a great job of planning for retirement, they still find an internal need to be active.

I see retirement activity in many forms. On the other hand, I have seen some retirees take the approach on retirement that life is about done and there is no need to learn something new or seek new challenges. I am very saddened when I see this attitude and it seems like some folks have just given up on life in general. Typically, this group of folks fulfill their own prophecy about the backside of life and don't get to experience this whole new, and potentially vibrant, season.

Health Care

Take a second to reflect on your health care plan. Although working up to or even past age sixty-five would allow you to avoid a coverage gap between your working years and Medicare, that may not be an option for you. Even if it is, when you retire, you will need to make some decisions about what kind of insurance coverage you may need to supplement your Medicare. Are there any medical needs you have that may require coverage in addition to Medicare? Did your parents or grandparents have any inherited medical conditions you might consider using a special savings plan to cover?

These are all questions that are important to review with your financial professional so you can be sure you have enough money put aside for health care.

Long-Term Care

Longevity means the need for long-term care is statistically more likely to happen. If you intend to pass on a legacy, planning for long-term care is paramount, since most estimates project nearly 70 percent of Americans will need some type of it.[6] However, this may be one of the biggest, most stressful pieces of longevity planning I encounter in my work. For one thing, who wants to talk about the point in their lives when they may feel the most limited? Who wants to dwell on what will happen if they no longer can toilet, bathe, dress, or feed themselves?

I get it; this is a less-than-fun part of planning. But a little bit of preparation now can go a long way!

When it comes to your longevity, just like with your goals, one of the important things to do is sit and dream. It may not be the fun, road-trip-to-the-Grand-Canyon kind of dreaming, but you can spend time envisioning how you want your twilight years to look.

For instance, if it is important for you to live in your home for as long as possible, who will provide for the day-to-day fixes and to-dos of housework if you become ill? Will you set aside money for a service, or do you have relatives or friends nearby whom you could comfortably allow to help you? Do you prefer in-home care over a nursing home or assisted living? This could be a good time to discuss the possibility of moving into a retirement community versus staying where you are or whether it's worth moving to another state and leaving relatives behind.

These are all important factors to discuss with your spouse and children, as *now* is the right time to address questions and concerns. For instance, is aging in place more important to one spouse than the other? Are the friends or relatives who live nearby emotionally, physically, and financially capable of helping you for a time if you face an illness?

Many families I meet with find these conversations very uncomfortable, particularly when children discuss nursing home care with their parents. A knee-jerk reaction for many is to promise they will care for their aging parents. This is noble and well-intentioned, but there needs to be an element of realism here. Does "help" from an adult child mean they stop

---

[6] LongTermCare.gov. February 18, 2020. "How Much Care Will You Need?" https://acl.gov/ltc/basic-needs/how-much-care-will-you-need

by and help you with laundry, cooking, home maintenance, and bills? Or does it mean they move you into their spare room when you have hip surgery? Are they prepared to help you use the restroom and bathe if that becomes difficult for you to do on your own?

I don't mean to discourage families from caring for their own; this can be a profoundly admirable relationship when it works out. However, I've seen families put off planning for late-in-life care based on a tenuous promise that the adult children would care for their parents, only to watch as the support system crumbles. Sometimes this is because the assumed caregiver hasn't given serious thought to the preparation they would need, both in a formal sense and regarding their personal physical, emotional, and financial commitments. This is often also because we can't see the future: Alzheimer's disease and other maladies of old age can exact a heavy toll. When a loved one reaches the point where he or she is at risk of wandering away or needs help with two or more activities of daily living, it can be more than one person or family can realistically handle.

If you know what you want, communicate with your family about both the best-case and worst-case scenarios. Then, hope for the best, and plan for the worst.

Realistic Cost of Care

Wrapped up in your planning should be a consideration for the cost of long-term care. One study estimates that by 2030, the nation's long-term care costs could reach $2.5 trillion as roughly 24 million Americans require some type of long-term care.[7] The potential costs for such care and treatment can be underestimated, especially by those who have maintained robust health and find it difficult to envision future declines to their condition.

---

[7] Tara O'Neill Hayes, Sara Kurtovic. Americanactionforum.org. February 18, 2020. "The Ballooning Costs of Long-Term Care." https://www.americanactionforum.org/research/the-ballooning-costs-of-long-term-care/

Another piece of planning for long-term care costs is anticipating inflation. It's common knowledge that prices have been and keep rising, which will lower your purchasing power on everything from food to medical care. Long-term care is a big piece of the inflation-disparity pie, which is part of why many find their estimates of nursing home care widely miss the mark. According to one survey, people expected to pay around $25,350 in annual out-of-pocket long-term care expenses, but, in reality, they'll more likely pay over $47,000.[8]

While local costs vary from state to state, here's the national median for various forms of long-term care (plus projections that account for a 3 percent annual inflation, so you can see what I am referencing):[9]

Long-Term Care Costs: Inflation				
	Home Health Care, Homemaker Services	Adult Day Care	Assisted Living	Nursing Home (semi-private room)
Annual 2021	$59,488	$20,280	$54,000	$94,900
Annual 2031	$79,947	$27,255	$72,571	$127,538
Annual 2041	$107,442	$36,628	$97,530	$171,400
Annual 2051	$144,393	$49,225	$131,072	$230,347

[8] Moll Law Group. 2021. "The Cost of Long-Term Care."
https://www.molllawgroup.com/the-cost-of-long-term-care.html
[9] Genworth Financial. June 2020. "Cost of Care Survey 2020."
https://www.genworth.com/aging-and-you/finances/cost-of-care.html

Fund Your Long-Term Care

One critical mistake I see are those who haven't planned for long-term care because they assume the government will provide everything. But that's a big misconception. The government has two health insurance programs: Medicare and Medicaid. These can greatly assist you in your health care needs in retirement but usually don't provide enough coverage to cover all your health care costs in retirement. My firm isn't a government outpost, so we don't get to make decisions when it comes to forming policy and specifics about either one of these programs. I'm going to give the overview of both, but if you want to dive into the details of these programs, you can visit www.Medicare.gov and www.Medicaid.gov.

Medicare

Medicare covers those aged sixty-five and older and those who are disabled. Medicare's coverage of any nursing-home-related health issues is limited. It might cover your nursing home stay if it is not a "custodial" stay, and it isn't long-term. For example, if you break a bone or suffer a stroke, stay in a nursing home for rehabilitative care, and then return home, Medicare may cover you. But, if you have developed dementia or are looking to move to a nursing facility because you can no longer bathe, dress, toilet, feed yourself, or take care of your hygiene, etc., then Medicare is not going to pay for your nursing home costs.[10]

You can enroll in Medicare anytime during the three months before and four months after your sixty-fifth birthday. Miss your enrollment deadline, and you could risk paying increased premiums for the rest of your life. On top of prompt enrollment, there are a few other things to think about when it comes to Medicare, not least among them being the need to understand the different "parts," what they do, and what they don't cover.

---

[10] Medicare.gov. "What Part A covers." https://www.medicare.gov/what-medicare-covers/part-a/what-part-a-covers.html

Part A

Medicare Part A is what you might think of as "classic" Medicare. Hospital care, some types of home health care, and major medical care fall under this. While most enrollees pay nothing for this service (as they likely paid into the system for at least ten years), you may end up paying, either based on work history or delayed signup. In 2022, the highest premium is $499 per month, and a hospital stay does have a deductible, $1,556.[11] And, if you have a hospital stay that surpasses sixty days, you could be looking at additional costs; keep in mind, Medicare doesn't pay for long-term care and services.

Part B

Medicare Part B is an essential piece of wrap-around coverage for Medicare Part A. It helps pay for doctor visits and outpatient services. This also comes with a price tag: Although the Part B deductible is only $233 in 2022, you will still pay 20 percent of all costs after that, with no limit on out-of-pocket expenses.[12]

Part C

Medicare Part C, more commonly known as Medicare Advantage plans, are an alternative to a combination of Parts A, B, and sometimes D. Administered through private insurance companies, these have a variety of costs and restrictions, and they are subject to the specific policies and rules of the issuing carrier.

---

[11] Medicare. "Medicare 2022 Costs at a Glance."
https://www.medicare.gov/your-medicare-costs/medicare-costs-at-a-glance
[12] Ibid.

Part D

Medicare Part D is also through a private insurer and is supplemental to Parts A and B, as its primary purpose is to cover prescription drugs. Like any private insurance plan, Part D has its quirks and rules that vary from insurer to insurer.

The Donut Hole

Even with a "Part D" in place, you may still have a coverage gap between what your Part D private drug insurance pays for your prescription and what basic Medicare pays. In 2022, the coverage gap is $4,430, meaning, after you meet your private prescription insurance limit, you will spend no more than 25 percent of your drug costs out-of-pocket before Medicare will kick in to pay for more prescription drugs.[13]

Medicare Supplements

Medicare Supplement Insurance, MedSup, Medigap, or plans labeled Medicare Part F, G, H, I, J . . . Known by a variety of monikers, this is just a fancy way of saying "medical coverage for those over sixty-five that picks up the tab for whatever the federal Medicare program(s) doesn't." Again, costs, limitations, etc., vary by carrier.

Does that sound like a bunch of government alphabet soup to you? It certainly does to me. And, did you read the fine print? Unpredictable costs, varied restrictions, difficult-to-compare benefits, donut holes, and coverage gaps. That's par for the course with health care plans through the course of our adult lives. What gives? I thought Medicare was supposed to be easier, comprehensive, and at no cost!

---

[13] Medicare. "Costs in the coverage gap."
https://www.medicare.gov/drug-coverage-part-d/costs-for-medicare-drug-coverage/costs-in-the-coverage-gap

The truth is there is no stage of life when health care is easy to understand.

The best thing you can do for yourself is to scope out the health care field early, compare costs often, and prepare for out-of-pocket costs well in advance—decades, if possible.

Medicaid

Medicaid is a program the states administer, so funding, protocol, and limitations vary. Compared to Medicare, Medicaid more widely covers nursing home care, but it targets a different demographic: those with low incomes.

If you have more assets than the Medicaid limit in your state and need nursing home care, you will need to use those assets to pay for your care. You will also have a list of additional state-approved ways to spend some of these assets over the Medicaid limit, such as pre-purchasing burial plots and funeral expenses or paying off debts. After that, your remaining assets fund your nursing home stay until they are gone, at which point Medicaid will jump in.

Some people aren't stymied by this, thinking they will just pass on their financial assets early, gifting them to relatives, friends, and causes so they can qualify for Medicaid when they need it. However, to prevent this exact scenario, Uncle Sam has implemented the look-back period. Currently, if you enroll in Medicaid, you are subject to having the government scrutinize the last five years of your finances for large gifts or expenses that may subject you to penalties, temporarily making you ineligible for Medicaid coverage.

So, if you're planning to preserve your money for future generations and retain control of your financial resources during your lifetime, you'll probably want to prepare for the costs of longevity beyond a "government plan."

Self-Funding

One way to fund a longer life is the old-fashioned way, through self-funding. There are a variety of financial tools you can use, and they all have their pros and cons. If your assets are in low-interest financial vehicles (savings, bonds, CDs), you risk letting inflation erode the value of your dollar. Or, if you are relying on the stock market, you have more growth potential, but you'll also want to consider the possible implications of market volatility. What if your assets take a hit? If you suffer a loss in your retirement portfolio in early or mid-retirement, you might have the option to "tighten your belt," so to speak, and cut back on discretionary spending to allow your portfolio the room to bounce back. But, if you are retired and depend on income from a stock account that just hit a downward stride, what are you going to do?

HSAs

These days, you might also be able to self-fund through a health savings account, or HSA, if you have access to one through a high-deductible health plan (you will not qualify to save in an HSA after enrolling in Medicare). In an HSA, any growth of your tax-deductible contributions will be tax-free, and any distributions paid out for qualified health costs are also tax-free. Long-term care expenses count as health costs, so, if this is an option available to you, it is one way to use the tax advantages to self-fund your longevity. Bear in mind, if you are younger than sixty-five, any money you use for nonqualified expenses will be subject to taxes and penalties, and, if you are older than sixty-five, any HSA money you use for non-medical expenses is subject to income tax.

LTCI

One slightly more nuanced way to pay for longevity, specifically for long-term care, is long-term care insurance, or LTCI. As car insurance protects your assets in case of a car accident and home insurance protects your assets in case something happens to your house, long-term care insurance aims to protect your assets in case you need long-term care in an at-home or nursing home situation.

As with other types of insurance, you will pay a monthly or annual premium in exchange for an insurance company paying for long-term care down the road. Typically, policies cover two to three years of care, which is adequate for an "average" situation: it's estimated 70 percent of Americans will need about three years of long-term care of some kind. However, it's important to consider you might not be "average" when you are preparing for long-term care costs; on average, 20 percent of today's sixty-five-year-olds could need care for longer than five years. [14]

Now, there are a few oft-cited components of LTCI that make it unattractive for some:

- Expense — LTCI can be expensive. It is generally less expensive the younger you are, but a fifty-five-year-old couple who purchased LTCI in 2022 could expect to pay $2,080 each year for an average three-year coverage policy. And the annual cost only increases from there the older you are. [15]

- Limited options — Let's face it: LTCI may be expensive for consumers, but it can also be expensive for companies that offer it. With fewer companies willing to take on that expense, this narrows the market, meaning opportunities to price shop for policies with different options or custom benefits are limited.

- If you know you need it, you might not be able to get it — Insurance companies offering LTCI are taking on a risk that you may need LTCI. That risk is the foundation

---

[14] LongTermCare.gov. February 18, 2020. "How Much Care Will You Need?" https://acl.gov/ltc/basic-needs/how-much-care-will-you-need
[15] American Association for Long-Term Care Insurance. January 12, 2022. "2022 National Long-Term Care Insurance Price Index." https://www.aaltci.org/long-term-care-insurance/learning-center/ltcfacts-2022.php

of the product—you may or may not need it. If you know you will need it because you have a dementia diagnosis or another illness for which you will need long-term care, you will likely not qualify for LTCI coverage.

- Use it or lose it—If you have LTCI and are in the minority of Americans who die having never needed long-term care, all the money you paid into your LTCI policy is gone.
- Possibly fluctuating rates—Your rate is not locked in on LTCI. Companies maintain the ability to raise or lower your premium amounts. This means some seniors face an ultimatum: Keep funding a policy at what might be a less affordable rate *or* lose coverage and let go of all the money they paid in so far.

After that, you might be thinking, "How can people possibly be interested in LTCI?" But let me repeat myself—as many as 70 percent of Americans will need long-term care. And, although only 8 percent of Americans have purchased LTCI, keep in mind the high cost of nursing home care. Can you afford $7,000 a month to put into nursing home care and still have enough left over to protect your legacy? This is a very real concern considering one set of statistics reported a two-in-three chance that a senior citizen will become physically or cognitively impaired in their lifetime.[16] So, not to sound like a broken record, but it is vitally important to have a plan in place to deal with longevity and long-term care if you intend to leave a financial legacy.

My wife Karen and I have been married almost forty years at the time this book was published and have owned a home most of that time. During all that time we have owned a home, we have bought and paid for homeowners insurance. Why have we done this? We would not find ourselves devastated in the event of a fire, tornado, or other terrible event happened.

---

[16] payingforseniorcare.com. 2022. "Long-Term Senior Care Statistics" https://www.payingforseniorcare.com/statistics

The odds that our house could be destroyed by fire are about 1 in 3,000.[17] I have never enjoyed paying those premiums to the insurance company, especially when things were tight raising a family and building a business. I often thought the odds were in my favor of our home not burning down. I found myself negotiating logic, and all the other obligations of responsibility for Karen and me. But I kept paying those premiums.

In 2012, we had a fire sweep through our neck of the woods that burned over 350 homes and structures. We found ourselves without our home and many of the memories that came along with almost thirty years of marriage. At this moment I fully understood the benefit of a good homeowners policy. I was so happy that I knew we could rebuild our home without suffering a major financial setback.

Just as with any insurance product, if we knew when disaster was about to strike, we would know exactly what kind of insurance to buy and when to buy it. That is why it is called insurance. We transfer the financial responsibility from my household to the big insurance company. Well, when it comes to anticipating a need for long-term care, our chances stand at roughly 70 percent once we turn sixty-five.[18] The odds are definitely not in our favor of growing old without having to deal with this issue.

I have dealt with long-term care needs for both my parents and have seen countless families have to cross this bridge. There are different ways to deal with this issue. Some are more expensive than others. Buying long-term care insurance is not the only solution, but it is a solution. There are ways to "leverage dollars" to provide for long-term care needs. The main thing is to devise a game plan.

A few relevant statistics to keep in mind:

---

[17] homex.com. 2022. "What Are The Odds Of A House Burning Down?" https://homex.com/ask/what-are-the-odds-of-a-house-burning-down
[18] LongTermCare.gov. February 18, 2020. "How Much Care Will You Need?" https://acl.gov/ltc/basic-needs/how-much-care-will-you-need

- The longer you live, the more likely you are to continue living; the longer you live, the more health care you will likely need to pay for.
- The average cost of a private nursing home room in the United States in 2020 was $8,821 a month.[19] But keep in mind, that is just the nursing home—it doesn't include other medical costs, let alone pleasantries, like entertainment or hobby spending.
- In 2020, Fidelity calculated that a healthy couple retiring at age sixty-five could expect to pay around $300,000 over the course of retirement to cover health and medical expenses.
- The average man will need $143,00, and the average woman needs about 10 percent more, or $157,000, because of women's longer life expectancies.[20]

I know. Whoa, there, Brian, I was hoping to have a realistic idea of health costs, not be driven over by a cement mixer!

The good news is, while we don't know these exact costs in advance, we know there *will* be costs. And you won't have to pay your total Medicare lifetime premiums in one day as a lump sum. Now that you have a good idea of health care costs in retirement, you can *plan* for them! That's the real point, here: Planning in advance can keep you from feeling nickel-and-dimed to your wits' end. Instead, having a sizeable portion of your assets earmarked for health care can allow you the freedom to choose health care networks, coverage options, and long-term care possibilities you like and that you think offer you the best in life.

---

[19] Genworth Financial. February 12, 2021. "Genworth 2020 Cost of Care Survey." https://www.genworth.com/aging-and-you/finances/cost-of-care.html

[20] Elizabeth O'Brien. Money. May 10, 2021. "Health Care Now Costs Couples $300,000 in Retirement, According to Fidelity's Latest Estimate." https://money.com/health-care-costs-retirement-fidelity-2021-study/

Product Riders

LTCI and self-funding are not the only ways to plan for the expenses of longevity. Some companies are getting creative with their products, particularly insurance companies. One way they are retooling to meet people's needs is through optional product riders on annuities and life insurance. Elsewhere in this book, I talk about annuity basics, but here's a brief overview: Annuities are insurance contracts. You pay the insurance company a premium, either as a lump sum or as a series of payments over a set amount of time, in exchange for guaranteed income payments. One of the advantages of an annuity is it has access to riders, which allow you to tweak your contract for a fee, usually about 1 percent of the contract value annually. One annuity rider some companies offer is a long-term care rider. If you have an annuity with a long-term care rider and are not in need of long-term care, your contract behaves as any annuity contract would—nothing changes. Generally speaking, if you reach a point when you can't perform multiple functions of daily life on your own, you notify the insurance company, and a representative will turn on those provisions of your contract.

Like LTCI, different companies and products offer different options. Some annuity long-term care riders offer coverage of two years in a nursing home situation. Others cap expenses at two times the original annuity's value. It greatly depends. Some people prefer this option because there isn't a "use-it-or-lose-it" piece; if you die without ever having needed long-term care, you still will have had the income benefit from the base contract. Still, as with any annuities or insurance contracts, there are the usual restrictions and limitations. Withdrawing money from the contract will affect future income payments, early distributions can result in a penalty, income taxes may apply, and, because the insurance company's solvency is what guarantees your payments, it's important to do your research about the insurance company you are considering purchasing a contract from.

Understandably, a discussion on long-term care is bound to feel at least a little tedious. Yet, this is a critical piece of planning for income in retirement, particularly if you want to leave a legacy.

I recall an uncomfortable discussion with a couple about long-term care planning. The big issue that came up was the pain of spending the money to provide protection. Even though there was money in the budget to buy coffee every day at five dollars a cup, enough money in the budget to dine out five to six times per week, enough money in the budget to vacation three to four times per year, enough money in the budget to have every premium cable television channel available, enough money in the budget to have a new car in the driveway for each of them, and the list goes on and on. Somehow, though, money proved tight to provide for the family in the case of a catastrophic event.

Unfortunately, as fate would have it, such an event happened. The husband who had planned to always be okay, had a sudden stroke in his mid-sixties. He was under the impression that if he were to get sick, his wife would be there to help take care of him. She was, yet she could detect an immediate problem. Her husband happened to be a good-sized fella. Soon, she realized that she could not lift him and get him into the bath. She could not move him from the bed to his wheelchair. She had trouble lifting him to help him get dressed. And again, the list went on and on.

She discovered she had to have help in facilitating his activities of daily living. She just could not do it by herself. This proved heart-wrenching. They loved each other very much and had been married for many years. They had always planned to be there for each other throughout their entire lives and they had been. They did not plan to fail; they just failed to plan. They did not take into consideration what the cost would be to have someone come to the home to just assist with the day-in and day-out activities of daily living. They had saved money for retirement so they could enjoy their "golden years." They just did not plan on spending a whole lifetime of savings in just a few short years.

Spousal Planning

Here's one thing to keep in mind no matter how you plan to save: Many of us will be planning for more than ourselves. Look back at all the stats on health events and the likelihood of long life and long-term care. If they hold true for a single individual, then the likelihood of having a costly health or long-term care event is even higher for a married couple. You'll be planning for not just one life, but two. So, when it comes to long-term care insurance, annuities, self-funding, or whatever strategy you are looking at using, be sure you are funding longevity for the both of you.

CHAPTER 2

Taxes

W here to begin with taxes? Perhaps by acknowledging we all bear responsibility for the resources we share. Roads, bridges, schools . . . It is the patriotic duty of every American to pay their fair share of taxes. Many would agree with me, though, while they don't mind paying their fair share, they're not interested in paying one cent more than that!

Now, just talking taxes probably takes your mind to April—tax season. You are probably thinking about all the forms you collect and how you file. Perhaps you are thinking about your certified public accountant or another qualified tax professional and saying to yourself, "I've already got taxes taken care of, thanks!"

However, what I see when people come into my office is that their relationship with their tax professional is purely a January through April relationship. That means they may have a tax professional who works only on income tax filing.

What I mean is tax planning extends beyond filing taxes. In April, we are required to settle our accounts with the IRS to make sure we have paid up on our bill or to even the score if we have overpaid. But real tax planning is about making each financial move in a way that allows you to keep the most money in your pocket and out of Uncle Sam's.

Now, as a caveat, I want to emphasize I am neither a CPA nor a tax planner, but I see the way taxes affect my clients, and I have plenty of experience helping clients implement tax-efficient strategies in their retirement plans in conjunction with their tax professionals.

Although I advocate tax-efficient strategies with my clients and understand the tax laws, I have learned through the years that I cannot be my own doctor. I have learned to understand the importance of working with other professionals who do what they do and have the experience and expertise in their profession. Although I could probably do much of my own taxes, I choose to not take the risk of being my own tax professional. I am not a CPA nor am I an in-depth expert on all the different situations that arise in the tax arena.

I have seen the need to work with a true tax professional that detects certain details I might overlook. Yes, I have to write the check for this expert advice, but the cost is much less expensive than the price I pay for doing it myself and having a tax mishap. I have seen this to be true for many of our clients. I have had multiple clients that have come to our firm over the years with self-inflicted tax oversights. In many cases, these issues could have been avoided with the help a good tax professional provides.

Again, a good tax professional is well worth the expense. Be sure to understand the difference between a good CPA and a tax preparer. A good CPA will work with you to become tax-efficient, while a run-of-the-mill tax preparer will calculate your taxes. The difference in the two can be consequential in terms of spotting potential tax issues in the future.

It is especially important to me to help my clients develop tax-efficient strategies in their retirement plans because each dollar they can keep in their pockets is a dollar we can put to work.

It is important to plan for tax diversification much like investment diversification. Just as we have proper asset allocation in our different investment strategies, when we plan our income streams for the distribution phase of assets during our retirement years, proper tax diversification can have a big impact on retirement income.

We want to find the sweet spot to satisfy income needs while avoiding potential tax problems that arise from taking income distributions from different buckets (tax and tax-free). Distributions can adversely affect your tax burden, including the taxes you pay on Social Security. We have already paid taxes on Social Security once when you paid into that system during your working years, and you can find yourself paying taxes on Social Security again without proper tax diversification while collecting your benefit.

The Fed

Now, in the United States, taxes can be a rather uncertain proposition. Depending on who is in the White House and which party controls Congress, we might be tempted to assume tax rates could either decline or increase in the next four to eight years accordingly. However, there is one (large!) factor we, as a nation, must confront: the national debt.

Currently, according to USDebtClock.org, we are over $29,000,000,000,000 in debt and climbing. That's $29 *trillion* with a "T." With just $1 trillion, you could park it in the bank at a zero percent interest rate and spend more than $54 million every day for fifty years without hitting a zero balance.

Even if Congress got a handle and stopped that debt from its daily compound, divided by each taxpayer, we each would owe about $214,000. So, will that be check, cash, or Venmo?

My point here isn't to give you anxiety. I'm just cautioning you that even with the rosiest of outlooks on our personal income tax rates, none of us should count on low tax rates for the long term. Instead, you and your network of professionals (tax, legal, and financial) should constantly be looking for ways to take advantage of tax-saving opportunities as they come. After all, the best "luck" is when proper planning meets opportunity.

So, how can we get started?

Know Your Limits

One of the foundational pieces of tax planning is knowing what tax bracket you are in, based on your income after subtracting pre-tax or untaxed assets. Your income taxes are based on your taxable income.

One reason to know your taxable income and your income tax rate is so you can see how far away you are from the next lower or higher tax bracket. This is particularly important when it comes to decisions such as gifting and Roth IRA rollovers.

For instance, based on the 2022 tax table, Mallory and Ralph's taxable income is just over $345,000, putting them in the 32 percent tax bracket and about $4.900 above the upper end of the 24 percent tax bracket. They have already maxed out their retirement funds' tax-exempt contributions for the year. Their daughter, Gloria, is a sophomore in college. This couple could shave a considerable amount off their tax bill if they use the $4,900 to help Gloria out with groceries and school—something they were likely to do, anyway, but now can deliberately be put to work for them in their overall financial strategy.

Now, I use Mallory and Ralph only as an example—your circumstances are probably different—but I think this nicely illustrates the way planning ahead for taxes can save you money.

Assuming a Lower Tax Rate

Many people anticipate being in a lower tax bracket in retirement. It makes sense: You won't be contributing to retirement funds; you'll be drawing from them. And you won't have all those work expenses—work clothes, transportation, lunch meetings, etc.

Yet, do you really plan on changing your lifestyle after retirement? Do you plan to cut down on the number of times you eat out, scale back vacations, and skimp on travel?

What I see in my office is many couples spend more in the first few years, or maybe the first decade, of retirement. Sure, that may taper off later on, but usually only just in time for their budget to be hit with greater health and long-term care expenses. Do you see where this is going? Many people plan as though their taxable income will be lower in retirement and are surprised when the tax bills come in and look more or less the same as they used to. It's better to plan for the worst and hope for the best, wouldn't you agree?

401(k)/IRA

One sometimes-unexpected piece of tax planning in retirement concerns your 401(k) or IRA. Most of us have one of these accounts or an equivalent. Throughout our working lives, we pay in, dutifully socking away a portion of our earnings in these tax-deferred accounts. There's the rub: tax-deferred. Not tax-free. Very rarely is anything free of taxation when you get down to it. Using 401(k)s and IRAs in retirement is no different. The taxes the government deferred when you were in your working years are now coming due, and you will pay taxes on that income at whatever your current tax rate is.

Just to ensure Uncle Sam gets his due, the government also has a required minimum distribution, or RMD, rule. Beginning at age seventy-two, you are required to withdraw a certain minimum amount every year from your 401(k) or IRA, or else you will face a 50 percent tax penalty on any RMD monies you should have withdrawn but didn't—and that's on top of income tax.

Of course, there is also the Roth IRA account. You can think of the difference between a Roth IRA and a traditional retirement account as the difference between taxing the seed and taxing the harvest. Because Roth IRAs are funded with post-tax dollars, there aren't tax penalties for early withdrawals of the principal nor are there taxes on the growth after you reach age fifty-nine-and-one-half. Perhaps best of all, there are no RMDs. Of course, you must own a Roth IRA account for a minimum of five years before you are able to take advantage of all its features.

This is one more area where it pays to be aware of your tax bracket. Some people may find it advantageous to "convert" their traditional retirement account funds to Roth IRA account funds in a year during which they are in a lower tax bracket. Others may opt to put any excess RMDs from their traditional retirement accounts into other products, like stocks or insurance.

Does that make your head spin? Understandable. That's why it's so important to work with a financial professional and tax planner who can help you not only execute these sorts of tax-efficient strategies but also help you understand what you are doing and why. [21]

---

[21] A Roth IRA conversion creates a taxable event that may not be right for everyone. Consult your tax advisor regarding your situation.

CHAPTER 3

Market Volatility

U p and down. Roller coaster. Merry-go-round. Bulls and bears. Peak-to-trough.

Sound familiar? This is the language we use to talk about the stock market. With volatility and spikes, even our language is jarring, bracing, and vivid.

Still, financial strategies tend to revolve around market-based products, for good reasons. For one thing, there is no other financial class that packs the same potential for growth, pound for pound, as stock-based products. Because of growth potential, inflation protection, and new opportunities, it may be unwise to avoid the market entirely.

However, along with the potential for growth is the potential for loss. Many of the people I see in my office come in still feeling a bit burned from the market drama of 2000 to 2010. That was a rough stretch, and many of us are once-bitten-twice-shy investors, right?

So how do we balance these factors? How do we try to satisfy both the need for protection and the need for growth?

For one thing, it is important to recognize the value of diversity. Now, I'm not just talking about the diversity of assets among different kinds of stocks, or even different kinds of stocks and bonds. That's only one kind of diversity; while important, both stocks and bonds, though different, are both still market-based products. Most market-based products, even within a diverse portfolio, tend to rise or lower as a whole, just like an incoming tide. Therefore, a portfolio diverse in only market-sourced products won't automatically protect your assets during times when the market declines.

In addition to the sort of "horizontal diversity" you have by purchasing a variety of stocks and bonds from different companies, I also suggest you think about "vertical diversity," or diversity among asset classes. This means having different product types, including securities products, bank products, and insurance products—with varying levels of growth potential, liquidity, and protection—all in accordance with your unique situation, goals, and needs.

I believe it is important to look at the different asset class types and make sure that the protected money portion of the portfolio is truly guarded and understand that the risk portion of the portfolio does indeed carry risk. There is definitely a line between protection and risk products.

We use a particular computer software tool designed to measure the specific volatility that an individual can stomach. Is very important to understand what your drawdown limits are individually, and the purpose behind your different buckets of money and what they are set up to facilitate within your retirement income plan. For example, income needs, asset protection, and legacy desires are some elements you could be trying to safeguard.

As we get closer to the backside of life, many of our clients find that the roller coaster of the market is not quite as tolerable as it used to be. It does not mean you cannot have market-based products, it just means that a satisfying balance between protection and risk is important to achieve.

The Color of Money

When you're looking at the overall diversity of your portfolio, part of the equation is knowing which products fit in what category: what has liquidity, what has protection, and what has growth potential.

Before we dive in, keep in mind these aren't absolutes. You might think of liquidity, growth, and protection as primary colors. While some products will look pretty much yellow, red, or blue, others will have a mix of characteristics, making them more green, orange, or purple.

Growth

I like to think of the growth category as red. It's powerful, it's somewhat volatile, and it's also the category where we have the greatest opportunities for growth and loss. Often, products in the growth category will have a good deal of liquidity but very little protection. These are our market-based products and strategies, and we think of them mostly in shades of red and orange, to designate their growth and liquidity. This is a good place to be when you're young—think fast cars and flashy leather jackets—but its allure often wanes as you move closer to retirement. Examples of "red" products include:

- Stocks
- Equities
- Exchange-traded funds
- Mutual funds
- Corporate bonds
- Real estate investment trusts
- Speculations
- Alternative investments

Liquidity

Yellow is my liquid category color. I typically recommend having at least enough yellow money to cover six months' to a year's worth of expenses in case of emergency. Yellow assets don't need a lot of growth potential; they just need to be readily available when we need them. The "yellow" category includes assets like:

- Cash

- Money market accounts

Protection

The color of protection, to me, is blue. Tranquil, peaceful, sure, even if it lacks a certain amount of flash. This is the direction I like to see people generally move toward as they're nearing retirement. The red, flashy look of stock market returns and the risk of possible overnight losses is less attractive as we near retirement and look for more consistency and reliability. While this category doesn't come with a lot of liquidity, the products here are backed by an insurance company, a bank, or a government entity. "Blue" products include things such as:

- Certificates of deposit (backed by banks)
- Government-based bonds (backed by the U.S. government)
- Life insurance (backed by insurance companies)
- Annuities (backed by insurance companies)

Through my years of investing and visiting with clients, the unique ability to help clients increase their overall wealth by using market-based products has been humbling. However, we have all heard the old saying that we do not want to put all our eggs in one basket.

This makes it important to achieve the kind of balance that provides protection of your portfolio as well as the potential upside of market gains. I have clients ask how we can have protection and the opportunity for reasonable growth. Well, the good news is solutions exist.

There are ways to create opportunities that allow for a reasonable growth on a portion of your money and still maintain guarantees for those who do not like the roller coaster ride a turbulent market creates.

For example, a fixed index annuity bases its performance on a specific market index such as the S&P 500 while not directly invested in that index. An FIA typically includes a participation rate and rate caps, which can reduce potential gains achieved by the specified market index. A minimum rate of return is also inherent to an FIA and can benefit the owner when the market index declines. I will explore fixed index annuities further in Chapter 7.[22]

Proper balance is the key! Most folks just want to have peace of mind knowing that they are going to be okay to live their retirement lifestyle freely without the worry that they are going to run out of money on the backside of life.

401(k)s

I want to take a second to specifically address a product many retirees will be using to build their retirement income: the 401(k) and other retirement accounts. Any of these retirement accounts (IRAs, 401(k)s, 403(b)s, etc.) are basically "tax wrappers." What do I mean by that? Well, depending on your plan provider, a 401(k) could include target-date funds, passively managed products, stocks, bonds, mutual funds, or even variable, fixed, and fixed index annuities, all collected in one place and governed by rules (a.k.a. the "tax wrapper"). These rules govern how much money you can put inside, what ways you can put it in, when you will pay taxes on it, and when you can take the money out. Inside the 401(k), each of the products inside the "tax wrapper" might have its own fees or commissions, in addition to the management fee you pay on the 401(k) itself.

Now, fees can be troublesome. You can't get something for nothing, and fees are how many financial companies and professionals make a living. Yet, it's important to recognize even a fee with a fraction of a percentage point is money out of your pocket—money that represents not just the one-time fee of today but also represents an opportunity cost. A $100,000

---

[22] Annuity guarantees rely on financial strength and claims-paying ability of issuing insurance company. Annuities are insurance products that may be subject to fees, surrender charges, and holding periods which vary by carrier. Annuities are not FDIC insured.

IRA that earns 6 percent over a twenty-five-year period without investment fees would earn $430,000. But if just a 0.5 percent fee got factored into that investment, the IRA would be worth $379,000 in twenty-five years, a $50,500 decrease.[23] For someone close to retirement, how much do you think fees may have cost over their lifetime?

Even for those close to retirement, it's important to look at management fees and assess if you think you're getting what you pay for. Over the course of ten years, those costs can add up, and you may have decades ahead of you in which you will need to rely on your assets.

Dollar-Cost Averaging

With 401(k)s and other market-based retirement products, when you are investing for the long term, dollar-cost averaging is a concept that can work in your favor. When the market is trending up, if you are consistently paying in money, month over month, great; your investments can grow, and you are adding to your assets. When the market takes a dip, no problem; your dollars buy more shares at a lower price. At some point, we hope the market will rebound, in which case your shares can grow and possibly be more valuable than they were before. This concept is what we call "dollar-cost averaging." While it can't ensure a profit or guarantee against losses, it's a time-tested strategy for investing in a volatile market.

However, when you are in retirement, this strategy may work against you. You may have heard of "reverse" dollar-cost averaging. Before, when the market lost ground, you were "bargain-shopping"; your dollars purchased more assets at a reduced price. When you are in retirement, you are no longer the purchaser; you are selling. So, in a down market, you have

23 Pam Krueger. Kiplinger.com. January 8, 2021. "How to Spot (and Squash) Nasty Fees That Hide in Your Investments" https://www.kiplinger.com/retirement/retirement-planning/602043/how-to-spot-and-squash-nasty-fees-that-hide-in-your

to sell more assets to make the same amount of money as what you made in a favorable market.

I've had lots of people step into my office to talk to me about this, emphasizing, "my advisor says the market always bounces back, and I have to just hold on for the long term."

There's some basis for this thinking; thus far, the market has always rebounded to higher heights than before. But this is no guarantee, and the prospect of potentially higher returns in five years may not be very helpful in retirement if you are relying on the income from those returns to pay this month's electric bill, for example.

It is very important to understand that if you are invested in market-based instruments, they are going to go up and they are going to go down. If you maintain proper balance between protection and risk solutions, you will have the opportunity to weather the storm when the inevitable market corrections happen.

Is There a "Perfect" Product?

To bring us back around to the discussion of protection, growth, and liquidity, the ideal product would be a "ten" in all three categories, right? Completely guaranteed, doubling in size every few years, and accessible whenever you want. Does such a product exist? Anyone who says "yes" is either ignorant or malevolent.

Instead of running in circles looking for that perfect product, the silver bullet, the unicorn of financial strategies, it's more important to circle back to the concept of a balanced, asset-diverse portfolio.

This is why your interests may be best served when you work with a trusted financial professional who knows what various financial products can do and how to use them in your personal retirement strategy.

We find it advantageous for our clients to have proper balance between protection and risk when it comes to inflationary planning. We have to see our assets grow at a reasonable rate just to keep up with inflation, which began climbing in 2021, causing prices to rise at the fastest rate seen in America in four decades.[24]

We have to plan for this, especially because of longevity trends we referenced earlier in the book. The ability to live longer is certainly a positive development, but longevity puts more strain on our buckets of money to last longer. To offset the incredibly low interest rate environment that we also had evidenced when this book was published and also stave off potential risks posed by inflation, we must use solutions that provide opportunities for satisfactory rates of return on investments.

---

[24] Rachel Siegel, Andrew Van Dam. The Washington Post. January 12, 2022. "December prices rise 7 percent compared with a year ago, as 2021 inflation reaches highest in 40 years"
https://www.washingtonpost.com/business/2022/01/12/december-cpi-inflation/

CHAPTER 4

Retirement Income

R etirement. For many of us, it's what we've saved for and dreamed of, pinning our hopes to a magical someday. Is that someday full of traveling? Is it filled with grandkids? Gardening? Maybe your fondest dream is simply never having to work again, never having to clock in or be accountable to someone else.

Your ability to do these things all hinges on *income*. Without the money to support these dreams, even a basic level of work-free lifestyle is unsustainable. That's why planning for your income in retirement is so foundational. But where do we begin?

It's easy to feel overwhelmed by this question. Some may feel the urge to amass a large lump sum and then try to put it all in one product—insurance, investments, liquid assets—to provide all the growth, liquidity, and income they need. Instead, I think you need a more balanced approach. After all, retirement planning isn't magic. Like I mention elsewhere, there is no single product that can be all things to all people (or even all things to one person). No approach works unilaterally for everyone. That's why it's important to talk to a financial professional who can help you lay down the basics and take you step-by-step through the process. Not only will you have the assurance you have addressed the areas you need to, but you will also have an ally who can help you break down the process and help keep you from feeling overwhelmed.

Sources of Income

Thinking of all the pieces of your retirement expenses might be intimidating. But, like cleaning out a junk drawer or revisiting that garage remodel, once you have laid everything out, you can begin to sort things into categories.

Once you have a good overall picture of where your expenses will lie, you can start stacking up the resources to cover them.

Social Security

Social Security is a guaranteed, inflation-protected federal insurance program playing a significant part in most of our retirement plans. From delaying until you've reached full retirement age or beyond to examining spousal benefits, as I discuss elsewhere in this book, there is plenty you can do to try to make the most of this monthly benefit. As with all your retirement income sources, it's important to consider how to make this resource stretch to provide the most bang and buck for your situation.

Pension

Another generally reliable source of retirement income for you might be a pension, if you are one of the lucky people who still has one.

If you don't have a pension, go ahead and skim on to the next section. If you do have a pension, keep on reading.

Because your pension can be such a central piece of your retirement income plan, you will want to put some thought into answering basic questions about it.

How well is your pension funded? Since the heyday of the pension plan, some companies and governments have neglected to fund their pension obligations, causing a persistent problem with this otherwise reliable asset. However, research conducted by the Pew Charitable Trusts showed a collective increase in assets exceeding half a trillion dollars in state retirement plans fueled by strong market investment returns in fiscal 2021. Pew's estimates that state retirement systems rose to 80 percent funding for the first time in 2008.[25]

Consider the factors at play, though. Pensions had been underfunded and gained a boost from strong market performance in 2021. What happens to the solvency of those pension funds if the market declines?

It can be worthwhile to keep tabs on your pension's health and know what your options are for withdrawing your pension. If you have already retired and made those decisions, this may be a foregone conclusion. If not, it pays to know what you can expect and what decisions you can make, such as taking spousal options to cover your husband or wife if he or she outlives you.

Also, some companies are incentivizing lump-sum payouts of pensions to reduce the companies' payment liabilities. If that's the case with your employer, talk to your financial professional to see if it might be prudent to do something like that or if it might be better to stick with lifetime payments or other options.

Your 401(k) and IRA

One "modern way" to save for retirement is in a 401(k) or IRA (or their nonprofit or governmental equivalents). These tax-advantaged accounts are, in my opinion, a poor substitute for pensions, but one of the biggest disservices we do to ourselves is to not take full advantage of them in the first place. According to one article, only 32 percent of Americans invest in a 401(k),

---

[25] pewtrusts.org. September 14, 2021. "The State Pension Funding Gap: Plans Have Stabilized in Wake of Pandemic" https://www.pewtrusts.org/en/research-and-analysis/issue-briefs/2021/09/the-state-pension-funding-gap-plans-have-stabilized-in-wake-of-pandemic

though 59 percent of employed Americans have access to a 401(k) benefit option.[26]

Also, if you have changed jobs over the years, do the work of tracking down any benefits from your past employers. You might have an IRA here or a 401(k) there; keep track of those so you can pull them together and look at those assets when you're ready to look at establishing sources of retirement income.

Do You Have...

- Life insurance?
- Annuities?
- Long-term care insurance?
- Any passive income sources?
- Stock and bond portfolios?
- Liquid assets? (What's in your bank account?)
- Alternative investments?
- Rental properties?

It's important, if you are going through the work of sitting with a financial professional, to look at your full retirement income picture and pull together *all* your assets, no matter how big or small. From the free insurance policy offered at your bank to the sizable investment in your brother-in-law's modestly successful furniture store, you want to have a good idea of where your money is.

I have one particular client family that had several elements in their financial mix. They had traditional IRAs, Roth IRAs, three different 401(k)s from different employers, inherited IRAs from deceased parents, 403(b)s from working with different school districts, certificates of deposits (CDs), cash values in their life insurance policies, real estate investments,

---

[26] Amin Dabit. personalcapital.com. April 1, 2021. "The Average 401k Balance by Age." https://www.personalcapital.com/blog/retirement-planning/average-401k-balance-age/

and traditional bank savings accounts. Once we combined all the different pieces, they were surprised to see what the big picture looked like.

This is why we use what we call our "Money Map," a condensed, one-page overall financial picture that allowed this family to see the big picture. In their case, the Money Map included income sources, overall balances differentiating products that incorporated risk breakdowns, liquidity options, real estate holdings, protection products (life insurance, survivor benefits, long term care solutions), and legacy planning, while incorporating the family's goals and objectives.

Once the collective information could be made into a visual Money Map and laid out in a simple illustrative manner, these clients then understood what their big picture looked like. It was like cleaning out the junk drawer in the kitchen. They knew that there were some good things in there, but they also knew that there were some things that were out-of-date and probably needed to go.

Cleaning and organizing a "financial junk drawer" can help consumers make better sense of their financial instruments and how they interact. Sometimes the totality of what has been accumulated can be surprising as aspiring retirees prepare and plan for the backside of life.

Retirement Income Needs

How much income will you need in retirement? How do you determine that? A lot of people work toward a random number, thinking, "If I can just have a million dollars, I'll be comfortable in retirement!" Don't get me wrong; it is possible to save up a lot of money and then retire in the hopes you can keep your monthly expenses lower than some set estimation. But I think this carries a general risk of running out of money. Instead, I work with my clients to find out what their current and projected income needs are and then work from there to see how we might cover any gaps between what they have and what they want.

Goals and Dreams

I like to start with your pie in the sky. Do you find yourself planning for your vacations more thoroughly than you do your retirement? It's not uncommon for Americans to spend more time planning our vacations than we spend planning our retirements. Maybe it's because planning a vacation is less stressful: Having a week at the beach go awry is, well, a walk on the beach compared to running out of money in retirement. Whatever the case, perhaps it would be better if you thought of your retirement as a vacation in and of itself—no clocking in, no boss, no overtime. If you felt unlimited by financial strain, what would you do?

Would an endless vacation for you mean Paris and Rome? Would it mean mentoring at children's clubs or serving at the local soup kitchen? Or maybe it would mean deepening your ties to those immediately around you—neighbors, friends, and family. Maybe it would mean more time to take part in the hobbies and activities you love. Have you been considering a second (or even third) act as a small-business owner, turning a hobby or passion into a revenue source?

This is your time to daydream and answer the question: If you could do anything, what would you do?

After that, it's a matter of putting a dollar amount on it. What are the costs of round-the-world travel? One couple I know said their highest priority in retirement was being able to take each of their grandchildren on a cross-country vacation every year. That's a pretty specific goal—one that is reasonably easy to nail down a budget for.

I had one client family that had the plans to retire early at the age of fifty-five. They wanted to spend time with each other because over the past thirty-five years they had been busy raising their children, working in their careers, and dealing with the day-to-day run of life. They wanted to take advantage of the blessing of good health and wanted to be financially prepared for the retirement they had dreamed about. In their plans they wanted to travel to the places they had on their bucket list, spend time around the house doing the things they loved doing at home, spend lots of time with their children and grandchildren, serve in their church and be involved with a certain ministry. Recreational interests could also move to the front burner as they worked out, played golf, and hiked together. Or, on the right day, they could simply relax and take it easy together.

They understood early on the importance of planning for the backside of life. In today's world, we can spend as much, if not more leisure time, in retirement than we did in our working years. The backside of life comes pretty quickly once your journey begins. You must have a game plan in place if you want to live out your dreams and goals. It just does not happen by accident. God has big plans for each of us and we must be great stewards of what He has provided.

Current Budget

Compiling a current expense report is one of the trickiest pieces of retirement preparation. Many people assume the expenses of their lives in retirement will be different—lower. After all, there will be no drive to work, no need for a formal wardrobe, and, perhaps most impactful of all, no more saving for retirement!

Yet, we often underestimate our daily spending habits. That's why I typically ask my clients to bring in their bank statements for the past year—they are reflective of your *actual* spending, not just what you think you're spending.

One of the first items of business when putting together a game plan for the backside of life is having an honest picture of what can be removed from your expenses. We have every client complete a budget worksheet that includes every dollar spent each month.

This includes EVERYTHING! I know that we all have unexpected expenses, which is why everyone should have an emergency fund. We know what our income versus expenses ratio looks like in our working years. We must also understand what that calculation looks like on the backside of life.

I can't count the number of times I have sat with a couple, asked them about their spending, and heard them throw out a number that seemed incredibly low. When I ask them where the number came from, they usually say they estimated based on their total bills. Yet, our spending is so much more than our mortgage, utilities, cable, phone, car, grocery, or credit card bills.

"What about clothes?" I ask, "Or dining out? What about gifts and coffees and last-minute birthday cards?" That's when the lights come on.

This is why I suggest collecting a year's worth of information. There is usually no such thing as a one-time purchase. Did you buy new furniture? Even if that is a rarity, do you think that will be the last time you *ever* buy furniture?

I remember sitting down with a couple and asking what their monthly budget looked like. They told me they spend about $4,000 per month. After I had them complete a budget worksheet that includes all the dollars going out EVERY MONTH, they came back to me and advised me that they discovered funds going out that they had not figured in their calculations.

The total amount going out was $6,300 per month. After completing a retirement analysis, this discrepancy projected they would run out of money much sooner in retirement than they had planned. This is not uncommon in the planning process. Remember, there is a myth out there that we don't need as much to live on during the backside of life as we did while working. I have not met a client who wants to reduce their standard of living the day they retire. We want to do the things on the backside of life that we have planned for now that we have the time and these things cost money.

Another hefty expense is spending on the kids. Many of the couples I work with are quick to help their adult children, whether it's something like letting them live in the basement, paying for college, babysitting, paying an occasional bill, or contributing to a grandchild's college fund. Research concluded that 22 percent of adults receive some kind of financial support from parents. That segment jumps to almost 30 percent when factoring the generation we call millennials.[27]

My clients sometimes protest that what they do for their grown children can stop in retirement. They don't *need* to help. But I get it. Parents like to feel needed. And, while you never want to neglect saving for retirement in favor of taking on financial risks (like your child's student debt), the parents who help their adult children do so in part because it helps them feel fulfilled.

When it comes down to expenses, including (and especially) spending on your family, don't make your initial calculations based on what you *could* whittle your budget down to if you *had* to. Instead, start from where you are. Who wants to live off a bare-bones bank account in retirement?

Other Expenses

Once you have nailed down your current budget and your dreams or goals for retirement, there are a few other outstanding pieces to think about—some expenses many people don't take the time to consider before making and executing a plan. But I'm assuming you want to get it right, so let's take a look.

---

[27] Kamaron McNair. magnifymoney.com. October 26, 2021. "Nearly 30% of Millenials Still Receive Financial Support From Their Parents" https://www.magnifymoney.com/blog/news/parental-financial-support-survey/

Housing

Do you know where you want to live in retirement? This makes up a substantial piece of your income puzzle—since the typical American household owns a home, and it's generally their largest asset.

Some people prefer to live right where they are for as long as they can. Others have been waiting for retirement to pull the trigger on an ambitious move, like purchasing a new house, or even downsizing. Whatever your plans and whatever your reasons, there are quite a few things to consider.

Mortgage

Do you still have a mortgage? What may have been a nice tax boon in your working years could turn into a financial burden in your retirement. After all, when you are on a limited income, a mortgage is just one more bill sapping your financial strength. It is something to put some thought into, whether you plan to age in place or are considering moving to your dream home, buying a house out of state, or living in a retirement community.

Upkeep and Taxes

A house without a mortgage still requires annual taxes. While it's tempting to think of this as a once-a-year expense, when you have limited earning potential, your annual tax bill might be something into which you should put a little more forethought.

The costs of homeownership aren't just monetary. When you find yourself dealing with more house than you need, it can drain your time and energy. From keeping clutter at bay to keeping the lawnmower running, upkeep can be extensive and expensive. For some, that's a challenge they heartily accept and can comfortably take on. For others, the idea of yard work or cleaning an area larger than they need feels foolish.

For instance, Peggy discovered after her knee replacement that most of her house was inaccessible to her when she was laid up.

"It felt ridiculous to pay someone else to dust and vacuum a house I was only living in 40 percent of!"

Practicality and Adaptability

Erik and Magda are looking to retire within the next two decades. They just sold their old three-bedroom ranch-style house. Their twins are in high school, and the couple has wanted to "upgrade" for years. Now they live in a gorgeous 1940s three-story house with all the kitchen space they ever wanted, five sprawling bedrooms, and a library and media room for themselves and their children. Within months of moving in, the couple realized a house perfect for their active teens would no longer be perfect for them in five to fifteen years.

"We are paying the mortgage for this house, but we've started saving for the next one," said Magda, "because who wants to climb two flights of stairs to their bedroom when they're seventy-eight?"

Others I know have encountered a similar situation in their personal lives. After a health crisis, one couple found the luxurious tub for two they toiled to install had become a specter of a bad slip and a potential safety risk. It's important to think through what your physical reality could be. I always emphasize to my clients that they should plan for whatever their long-term future might hold, but it's amazing how many people don't give it much thought.

Contracts and Regulations

If you are looking into a cross-country move, be aware of new tax tables or local ordinances in the area where you are looking to move. After all, you don't want to experience sticker-shock when you are looking at downsizing or reducing your bills in retirement.

Along the same lines, if you are moving into a retirement community, be sure to look at the fine print. What happens if you must move into a different situation for long-term care? Will you be penalized? Will you be responsible for replacing your slot in the community? What are all the fees, and what do they cover?

Inflation

As I write this in 2022, America has experienced a wave of inflation following a lengthy period of low inflation. Inflation zoomed to 9.1 percent in June 2022, its highest mark in more than forty years..[28] In particular, food prices pained Americans at the checkout line because of a 10.9 percent inflation rate, the largest increase for groceries since May 1979.[29]

However, inflation isn't a one-time bump; it has a cumulative effect. Again, that can impact the price of groceries greater than other goods. Even with relatively low inflation over the past few decades, the jar of peanut butter you bought in 1997 for $2.48 will cost $4.18 today. A $100 ticket to a 1997 sporting event now costs $221.11.[30] Some of you might choose to watch from home and feel better about eating your peanut butter sandwich.

What if, in retirement, we hit a stretch like the late seventies and early eighties, when annual inflation rates of 10 percent became the norm? It may be wise to consider some extra padding in your retirement income plan to account for any potential increase in inflation in the future.

---

[28] tradingeconomics.com. 2022 Data/2023 Forecast/1914-2021 Historical. "United States Inflation Rate" https://tradingeconomics.com/united-states/inflation-cpi

[29] tradingeconomics.com. August 2022. "United States Inflation Rate" https://tradingeconomics.com/united-states/inflation-cpi

[30] Ibid.

Aging

Also, in the expense category, think about longevity. We all hope to age gracefully. However, it's important to face the prospect of aging with a sense of realism.

The elephant in the room for many families is long-term care: No one wants to admit they will likely need it, but estimates say as many as 70 percent of us will.[31] Aging is a significant piece of retirement income planning because you'll want to figure out how to set aside money for your care, either at home or away from it. The more comfortable you get with discussing your wishes and plans with your loved ones, the easier planning for the financial side of it can be.

I discuss health care and potential long-term care costs in more detail elsewhere in this book, but suffice it to say nursing home care tends to be very expensive and typically isn't something you get to choose when you will need.

It isn't just the costs of long-term care that pose a concern in living longer. It's also about covering the possible costs of everything else associated with living longer. For instance, if Henry retires from his job as a biochemical engineer at age sixty-five, perhaps he planned to have a very decent income for twenty years, until age eighty-five. But what if he lives until he's ninety-five? That's a whole third—ten years—more of personal income he will need.

Putting It All Together

Whew! So, you have pulled together what you have, and you have a pretty good idea of where you want to be. Now your financial professional and you can go about the work of arranging what assets you *have* to cover what you *need*—and how you might try to cover any gaps.

---

31 Moll Law Group. 2021. "The Cost of Long-Term Care." https://www.molllawgroup.com/the-cost-of-long-term-care.html

Like the proverbial man in the Bible who built his house on a rock, I like to help my clients figure out how to cover their day-to-day living expenses—their needs—with insurance and other guaranteed income sources like pensions and Social Security.

When I visit with folks that have the backside of life threshold in their sights, we look at the big picture of what is coming into their bank account on a monthly basis against what is going out. We try to keep this calculation simplistic, thought unknown variables must be factored into the equation.

We have tools that help us include these unknown variables such as taxes, inflation, and investment risk. We use a retirement analyzer tool along with our Money Map to help incorporate these unknown variables into any budgeting exercise to provide a better financial outlook for the backside of life.

Again, you should keep in mind there isn't one single financial vehicle, asset, or source to fill all your needs, and that's okay. One of the challenges of planning for your income in retirement concerns figuring out what products and strategies to use. You can release some of that stress when you accept the fact you will probably need a diverse portfolio—potentially with bonds, stocks, insurance, and other income sources—not just one massive money pile.

One way to help shore up your income gaps is by working with your financial professional and a qualified tax advisor to mitigate your tax exposure. If you have a 401(k) or IRA, a tax advisor in your corner can help you figure out how and when to take distributions from your account in a way that doesn't push you into a higher tax bracket. Or you might learn how to use tax-advantaged bonds more effectively. Effective tax planning isn't necessarily about "adding" to your income. Especially regarding retirement, it's less about what you make than it is about what you keep. Paying a lower tax bill keeps more money in your pocket, which is where you want it when it comes to retirement income.

Now you can look at ways to cover your remaining retirement goals. Are there products like long-term care insurance specific to a certain kind of expense you anticipate? Is there a particular asset you want to use for your "play" money—money for trips and gifts for the grandkids? Is there any way you can portion off money for those charitable legacy plans?

Once you have analyzed your income wants, needs, and the assets to realistically cover them, you may have a gap. The masterstroke of a competent financial professional will be to help you figure out how you will cover that gap. Will you need to cut out a round of golf a week? Maybe skip the new car? Or will you need to take more substantial action?

One way to cover an income gap is to consider working longer or even part-time before retirement and even after that magical calendar date. This may not be the best "plan" for you; disabilities, work demands, and physical or emotional limitations can hinder the best-laid plans to continue working. However, if it is physically possible for you, this is one considerable way to help your assets last, for more than one reason.

In fact, 46 percent of the Americans responding to a survey report they plan to work part-time after retiring, while 18 percent indicated they planned to work past the age of seventy.[32]

Much work and planning goes into providing an adequate answer to the age-old question: "Can we retire and do we have enough?"

We hope that transitioning into the backside of life is a joyous moment in which confidence can be gained from knowing that an adequate framework has been developed for income retirees will need.

---

[32] Palash Ghosh. Forbes.com. May 6, 2021. "A Third Of Seniors Seek To Work Well Past Retirement Age, Or Won't Retire At All, Poll Finds" https://www.forbes.com/sites/palashghosh/2021/05/06/a-third-of-seniors-seek-to-work-well-past-retirement-age-or-wont-retire-at-all-poll-finds/?sh=1d2ece836b95

When you're retired, you no longer have an employer paying you a steady check. It is up to you to make sure you have saved and planned for the income you need.

CHAPTER 5

Social Security

Social Security is often the foundation of retirement income. Backed by the strength of the U.S. Treasury, it provides perhaps the most dependable paycheck you will have in retirement.

From the time you collect your first paycheck from the job that made you a bonafide taxpayer (for me, it was working at a Sonic Drive-In in Brownwood, Texas, when I was thirteen and spending the summer with my grandmother), you are paying into the grand old Social Security system. What grew and developed out of the pressures of the Great Depression has become one of the most popular government programs in the country, and, if you pay in for the equivalent of ten years or more, you, too, can benefit from the Social Security program.

Now, before we get into the nitty-gritty of Social Security, I'd like to address a current concern: Will Social Security still be there for you when you reach retirement age?

The Future of Social Security

This question is ever-present as headlines trumpet an underfunded Social Security program, alongside the sea of baby boomers who are retiring in droves and the comparatively smaller pool of younger people who are bearing the responsibility of funding the system.

The Social Security Administration itself acknowledges this concern as each Social Security statement now bears an asterisk that continues near the end of the summary:

"*Your estimated benefits are based on current law. Congress has made changes to the law in the past and can do so at any time. The law governing benefit amounts may change because, by 2034, the payroll taxes collected will be enough to pay only about 79 percent of scheduled benefits."

Just a reminder, as if you needed one, that nothing in life is guaranteed. Additionally, depending on who you're listening to, Social Security funds may run low before 2034 thanks to the financial instability and government spending that accompanied the 2020 COVID-19 pandemic.

Before you get too discouraged, though, here are a few thoughts to keep you going:

- Even if the program is only paying 79 cents on the dollar for scheduled benefits, 79 percent is notably not zero.
- The Social Security Administration has made changes in the distant and near past to protect the fund's solvency, including increasing retirement ages and striking certain filing strategies.
- There are many changes Congress could make, and lawmakers are currently discussing how to fix the system, such as further increasing full retirement age and eligibility.
- One thing no one is seriously discussing? Reneging on current obligations to retirees or the soon-to-retire.

Take heart. The real answer to the question, "Will Social Security be there for me?" is still yes.

This question is an important one to consider when you look at how much we, as a nation, rely on this program. Did you know Social Security benefits replace about 40 percent of a person's original income when they retire?[33]

If you ask me, that's a pretty significant piece of your retirement income puzzle.

Another caveat? You may not realize this, but no one can legally "advise" you about your Social Security benefits.

"But, Brian," you may be thinking, "isn't that part of what you do? And what about that nice gentleman at the Social Security Administration office I spoke with on the phone?"

Don't get me wrong. Social Security Administration employees know their stuff. They are trained to understand policies and programs, and they are usually pretty quick to tell you what you can and cannot do. But the government specifically stipulates, because Social Security is a benefit you alone have paid into and earned, your Social Security decisions, too, are yours alone.

When it comes to financial professionals, we can't push you in any directions, either, *but*—there's a big but here—working with a well-informed financial professional is still incredibly handy when it comes to your Social Security decisions. Why? Because someone who's worth his or her salt will know what withdrawal strategies might pertain to your specific situation and will ask questions that can help you determine what you are looking for when it comes to your Social Security.

For instance, some people want the highest possible monthly benefit. Others want to start their benefits early, not always because of financial need. I heard about one man who called in to start his Social Security payments the day he qualified, just because he liked to think of it as the government paying back a debt it owed him, and he enjoyed the feeling of receiving a check from Uncle Sam.

Whatever your reasons, questions, or feelings regarding Social Security, the decision is yours alone; but working with a

---

33 ssa.gov. "Alternate Measure of Replacement Rates for Social Security Benefits and Retirement Income"
https://www.ssa.gov/policy/docs/ssb/v68n2/v68n2p1.html.

financial professional can help you put your options in perspective by showing you—both with industry knowledge and with proprietary software or planning processes—where your benefits fit into your overall strategy for retirement income.

One reason the federal government doesn't allow for "advice" related to Social Security, I suspect, is so no one can profit from giving you advice related to your Social Security benefit—or from providing any clarifications. Again, this is a sign of a good financial professional. Those who are passionate about their work will be knowledgeable about what benefit strategies might be to your advantage and will happily share those possible options with you.

Full Retirement Age

When it comes to Social Security, it seems like many people only think so far as "yes." They don't take the time to understand the various options available. Instead, because it is common knowledge you can begin your benefits at age sixty-two, that's what many of us do. While more people are opting to delay taking benefits, age sixty-two is still firmly the most popular age to start.[34]

What many people fail to understand is, by starting benefits early, they may be leaving a lot of money on the table. You see, the Social Security Administration bases your monthly benefit on two factors: your earnings history and your Full Retirement Age (FRA).

From your earnings history, they pull the thirty-five years you made the most money and use a mathematical indexing formula to figure out a monthly average from those years. If you paid into the system for less than thirty-five years, then every year you didn't pay in will be counted as a zero.

---

[34] Chris Kissell. moneytalknews.com. January 20, 2021. "This Is When the Most People Start Taking Social Security." https://www.moneytalksnews.com/the-most-popular-age-for-claiming-social-security/

Once they have calculated what your monthly earning would be at FRA, the government then calculates what to put on your check based on how close you are to FRA. FRA was originally set at sixty-five, but, as the population aged and lifespans lengthened, the government shifted FRA later and later, based on an individual's year of birth. Check out the following chart to see when you will reach FRA.[35]

[35] Social Security Administration. "Full Retirement Age."
https://www.ssa.gov/planners/retire/retirechart.html

Age to Receive Full Social Security Benefits*	
(Called "full retirement age" [FRA] or "normal retirement age.")	
Year of Birth*	FRA
1937 or earlier	65
1938	65 and 2 months
1939	65 and 4 months
1940	65 and 6 months
1941	65 and 8 months
1942	65 and 10 months
1943-1954	66
1955	66 and 2 months
1956	66 and 4 months
1957	66 and 6 months
1958	66 and 8 months
1959	66 and 10 months
1960 and later	67

If you were born on Jan. 1 of any year, you should refer to the previous year. (If you were born on the 1st of the month, we figure your benefit [and your full retirement age] as if your birthday was in the previous month.)

When you reach FRA, you are eligible to receive 100 percent of whatever the Social Security Administration says is your full monthly benefit.

Starting at age sixty-two, for every year before FRA you claim benefits, your monthly check is reduced by 5 percent or more. Conversely, for every year you delay taking benefits past FRA, your monthly benefit increases by 8 percent (until age seventy—after that, there is no monetary advantage to delaying Social Security benefits). While your circumstances and needs may vary, a lot of financial professionals still urge people to at least consider delaying until they reach age seventy.

Why wait?[36]

Taking benefits early could affect your monthly check by _____.								
62	63	64	65	FRA 66	67	68	69	70
-25%	-20%	-13.3%	-6.7%	0	+8%	+16%	+24%	+32%

My Social Security

If you are over age thirty, you have probably received a notice from the Social Security Administration telling you to activate something called "My Social Security." This is a handy way to learn more about your particular benefit options, to keep track of what your earnings record looks like, and to calculate the benefits you have accrued over the years.

Essentially, My Social Security is an online account you can activate to see what your personal Social Security picture looks like, which you can do at www.ssa.gov/myaccount. This can be extremely helpful when it comes to planning for income in retirement and figuring up the difference between your anticipated income versus anticipated expenses.

---

[36] Social Security Administration. April 2021. "Can You Take Your Benefits Before Full Retirement Age?" https://www.ssa.gov/planners/retire/applying2.html

My Social Security is also helpful because it's a great way to see if there is a problem. For instance, I have heard of one woman who, through diligently checking her tax records against her Social Security profile, discovered her Social Security check was shortchanging her, based on her earnings history. After taking the discrepancy to the Social Security Administration, they sent her what they owed her in makeup benefits.

COLA

Social Security is a largely guaranteed piece of the retirement puzzle: If you get a statement that reads you should expect $1,000 a month, you can be sure you will receive $1,000 a month. But there is one variable detail, and that is something called the cost-of-living adjustment, or COLA.

The COLA is an increase in your monthly check meant to address inflation in everyday life. After all, your expenses will likely continue to experience inflation in retirement, but you will no longer have the opportunity for raises, bonuses, or promotions you had when you were working. Instead, Social Security receives an annual cost-of-living increase tied to the Department of Labor's Consumer Price Index for Urban Wage Earners and Clerical Workers, or CPI-W. If the CPI-W measurement shows inflation rose a certain amount for regular goods and services, then Social Security recipients will see that reflected in their COLA.

The COLA averages 4 percent, but in a no- or low-inflation environment, such as in 2010, 2011, and 2016, Social Security recipients will not receive an adjustment. Some view the COLA as a perk, bump, or bonus, but, in reality, it works more like this: Your mom sends you to the store with $2.50 for a gallon of milk. Milk costs exactly $2.50. The next week, you go back with that same amount, but it is now $2.52 for a gallon, so you go back to Mom, and she gives you 2 cents. You aren't bringing home more milk—it just costs more money.

So the COLA is less about "making more money" and more about keeping seniors' purchasing power from eroding when inflation is a big factor, such as in 1975, when it was 8 percent![37] Still, don't let that detract from your enthusiasm about COLAs; after all, what if Mom's solution was: "Here's the same $2.50; try to find pennies from somewhere else to get that milk!"?

Spousal Benefits

We've talked about FRA, but another big Social Security decision involves spousal benefits.

If you or your spouse has a long stretch of zeros in your earnings history—perhaps if one of you stayed home for years, caring for children or sick relatives—you may want to consider filing for spousal benefits instead of filing on your own earnings history. A spousal benefit can be up to 50 percent of the primary wage earner's benefit at full retirement age.

To begin drawing a spousal benefit, you must be at least sixty-two years old, and the primary wage earner must have already filed for his or her benefit. While there are penalties for taking spousal benefits early (you could lose up to 67.5 percent of your check for filing at age sixty-two), you cannot earn credits for delaying past full retirement age.[38]

Like I wrote, the spousal benefit can be a big deal for those who don't have a very long pay history, but it's important to weigh your own earned benefits against the option of withdrawing based on a fraction of your spouse's benefits.

To look at how this could play out, let's use a hypothetical couple: Mary Jane, who is sixty, and Peter, who is sixty-two.

Let's say Peter's benefit at FRA, in his case sixty-six, would be $1,600. If Peter begins his benefits right now, four years before FRA, his monthly check will be $1,200. If Mary Jane

---

[37] Social Security Administration. "Cost-Of-Living Adjustment (COLA) Information for 2021." https://www.ssa.gov/cola/
[38] Social Security Administration. "Retirement Planner: Benefits For You As A Spouse." https://www.ssa.gov/planners/retire/applying6.html

begins taking spousal benefits in two years at the earliest date possible, her monthly benefits will be reduced by 67.5 percent, to $520 per month (remember, at FRA, the most she can qualify for is half of Peter's FRA benefit).

What if Peter and Mary Jane both wait until FRA? At sixty-six, Peter begins taking his full benefit of $1,600 a month. Two years later, when she reaches age sixty-six, Mary Jane will qualify for $800 a month. By waiting until FRA, the couple's monthly benefit goes from $1,720 to $2,400.

What if Peter delays until age seventy to get his maximum possible benefit? For each year past FRA he delays, his monthly benefits increase by 8 percent. This means, at seventy, he could file for a monthly benefit of $2,112. However, delayed retirement credits do not affect spousal benefits, so as soon as Peter files at seventy, Mary Jane would also file (at age sixty-eight) for her maximum benefit of $800, so their highest possible combined monthly check is $2,912.[39]

When it comes to your Social Security benefits, you obviously will want to consider whether a monthly check based on a fraction of your spouse's earnings will be comparable to or larger than your own earnings history.

Divorced Spouses

There are a few considerations for those of us who have gone through a divorce. If you 1) were married for ten years or more *and* 2) have since been divorced for at least two years *and* 3) are unmarried *and* 4) your ex-spouse qualifies to begin Social Security, you qualify for a spousal benefit based on your ex-husband or ex-wife's earnings history at FRA. A divorced spousal benefit is different from the married spousal benefit in

---

[39] Office of the Chief Actuary. Social Security Administration. "Social Security Benefits: Benefits for Spouses." https://www.ssa.gov/OACT/quickcalc/spouse.html#calculator

one way: You don't have to wait for your ex-spouse to file before you can file yourself.[40]

For instance, Charles and Moira were married for fifteen years before their divorce, when he was thirty-six and she was forty. Moira has been remarried for twenty years, and, although Charles briefly remarried, his second marriage ended after a few years. Charles' benefits are largely calculated based on his many years of volunteering in schools, meaning his personal monthly benefit is close to zero.

Although Moira has deferred her retirement, opting to delay benefits until she is seventy, Charles can begin taking benefits calculated from Moira's work history at FRA as early as sixty-two. However, he will also have the option of waiting until FRA to collect the maximum, or 50 percent of Moira's earned monthly benefit at her FRA.

Widowed Spouses

If your marriage ended with the death of your spouse, you might claim a benefit for your spouse's earned income as his or her widow/widower, called a survivor's benefit. Unlike a spousal benefit or divorced benefits, if your husband or wife dies, you can claim his or her full benefit. Also, unlike spousal benefits, if you need to, you can begin taking income when you turn sixty. However, as with other benefit options, your monthly check will be permanently reduced for withdrawing benefits before FRA.

If your spouse began taking benefits before he or she died, you can't delay withdrawing your survivor's benefits to get delayed credits. The Social Security Administration maintains

---

[40] Social Security Administration. "Retirement Planner: If You Are Divorced." https://www.ssa.gov/planners/retire/divspouse.html

you can only get as much from a survivor's benefit as your deceased spouse might have received, had he or she lived.[41]

Taxes, Taxes, Taxes

With Social Security, as with everything, it is important to consider taxes. It may be surprising, but your Social Security benefits are not tax-free. Despite having been taxed to accrue those benefits in the first place, you may have to pay Uncle Sam income taxes on up to 85 percent of your Social Security.

The Social Security Administration figures these taxes using what they call "the provisional income formula." Your provisional income formula differs from the adjusted gross income you use for your regular income taxes. Instead, to find out how much of your Social Security benefit is taxable, the Social Security Administration calculates it this way:

Provisional Income = Adjusted Gross Income + Nontaxable Interest + ½ of Social Security

See that piece about nontaxable interest? That generally means interest from government bonds and notes. It surprises many people that, although you may not pay taxes on those assets, their income will count against you when it comes to Social Security taxation.

Once you have figured out your provisional income (also called "combined income"), you can use the following chart to figure out your Social Security taxes.[42]

---

[41] Social Security Administration. "Social Security Benefit Amounts For The Surviving Spouse By Year Of Birth."
https://www.ssa.gov/planners/survivors/survivorchartred.html
[42] Social Security Administration. "Benefits Planner: Income Taxes and Your Social Security Benefits." https://www.ssa.gov/planners/taxes.html

Taxes on Social Security		
Provisional Income = Adjusted Gross Income + Nontaxable Interest + ½ of Social Security		
If you are ____ and your provisional income is____, then...		Uncle Sam will tax ___ of your Social Security
Single	Married, filing jointly	
Less than $25,000	Less than $32,000	0%
$25,000 to $34,000	$32,000 to $44,000	Up to 50%
More than $34,000	More than $44,000	Up to 85%

This is one more reason it may benefit you to work with financial and tax professionals: They can look at your entire financial picture to make your overall retirement plan as tax-efficient as possible—including your Social Security benefit.

In the planning process in preparation for the backside of life, it is important that folks have different tax diversification buckets. You might consider converting traditional qualified funds to Roth accounts.

This creates a future tax-free bucket of money that can provide a tax-free income source that will help keep the taxable income amount lower. (These funds are tax-free once you reach age fifty-nine-and-one-half and the account has been open for at least five years). Understand that a Roth conversion is a taxable event. Federal taxes must be paid on the value of pre-tax contributions, as well as earnings on the traditional IRA in the year of the conversion. If your taxable income is lower as noted in the above chart, the amount of tax paid on your Social Security diminishes as well. It is important to manage the flows of income efficiently.

Working and Social Security:
The Earnings Test

If you haven't reached FRA, but you started your Social Security benefits and are still working, things get a little hairy.

Because you have started Social Security payments, the Social Security Administration will pay out your benefits (at that reduced rate, of course, because you haven't reached your FRA). Yet, because you are working, the organization must also withhold from your check to add to your benefits, which you are already collecting. See how this complicates matters?

To address the situation, the government has what is called the earnings test. For 2022, you can earn up to $19,560 without it affecting your Social Security check. But, for every $2 you earn past that amount, the Social Security Administration will withhold $1. The earnings test loosens in the year of your FRA; if you are reaching FRA in 2022, you can earn up to $51,960 before you run into the earnings test, and the government only withholds $1 for every $3 past that amount. The month you reach FRA, you are no longer subject to any earnings withholding. For instance, if you are still working and will turn sixty-six on December 28, 2022, you would only have to worry about the earnings test until December, and then you can ignore it entirely. Keep in mind, the money the government withholds from your Social Security benefits while you are working before FRA will be tacked back onto your benefits check after FRA.[43]

At our firm, we provide an in-depth Social Security analysis that will illustrate your benefits at different ages. It will project which option could provide the highest amount of Social Security dollars to you over your life expectancy.

What we do not know is when are we going to take our last breath of life. If we have longevity on our side, it may be better

---

[43] Social Security Administration. "Exempt Amounts Under the Earnings Test." https://www.ssa.gov/oact/cola/rtea.html

to defer taking our Social Security payments later on. If we do not have longevity on our side and have personal issues going that lead to a shorter life expectancy, it may be better to take your benefits earlier.

It is also important to calculate your anticipated retirement date and income streams available at various intervals. The earlier you start taking Social Security benefits, the lower amount of benefit will be paid. This decision is typically irreversible, so the lower payment is in effect for your entire lifetime.

CHAPTER 6

401(k)s & IRAs

Have you heard? Today's retirement is not your parents' retirement. You see, back in the day, it was pretty common to work for one company for the vast majority of your career and then retire with a gold watch and a pension.

The gold watch was a symbol of the quality time you had put in at that company, but the pension was more than a symbol. Instead, it was a guarantee—as solid as your employer—that they would repay your hard work with a certain amount of income in your old age. Did you see the caveat there? Your pension's guarantee was *as solid as your employer.* The problem was, what if your employer went under?

Companies that failed couldn't pay their retired employees' pensions, leading to financial challenges for many. Beginning in 1974 with Congress' passage of the Employee Retirement Income Security Act, federal legislation and regulations aimed at protecting retirees were everywhere. One piece of legislation included a relatively obscure section of the Internal Revenue Code, added in 1978. Section 401(k), to be specific.

IRC section 401, subsection k, created tax advantages for employer-sponsored financial products, even if the main contributor was the employee him or herself. Over the years, more employers took note, beginning an age of transition away from pensions and toward 401(k) plans. A 401(k) is a retirement account with certain tax benefits and restrictions on the investments or other financial products inside of it.

Essentially, 401(k)s and their individual retirement account (IRA) counterparts are "wrappers" that provide tax benefits around assets; typically, the assets that compose IRAs and 401(k)s are mutual funds, stock and bond mixes, and money market accounts. However, IRA and 401(k) contents are becoming more diverse these days, with some companies offering different kinds of annuity options within their plans.

Where pensions are defined-*benefit* plans, 401(k)s and IRAs are defined-*contribution* plans. The one-word change outlines the basic difference. Pensions spell out what you can expect to receive from the plan but not necessarily how much money it will take to fund those benefits. With 401(k)s, an employer sets a standard for how much they will contribute (if any), and you can be certain of what you are contributing. Still, there is no outline for what you can expect to receive in return for those contributions.

Modern employment looks very different. A 2018 survey by the Bureau of Labor Statistics determined U.S. workers stayed with their employers a median of about four years. Workers ages fifty-five to sixty-four had a little more staying power and were most likely to stay with their employer for about ten years.[44] Participation in 401(k) plans has steadily risen this century, totaling $7.3 trillion in assets in 2021 compared to $3.1 trillion in 2011. About 60 million active participants engaged in 401(k) plans in 2020.[45]

Those statistics make it clear that 401(k) plans have, at many companies, replaced pensions and for that matter, a gold watch.

Planning for retirement if you have a pension is is much different than planning for retirement without a pension. With

---

[44] Bureau of Labor Statistics. September 22, 2020. "Employee Tenure Summary." https://www.bls.gov/news.release/tenure.nr0.htm
[45] Investment Company Institute. October 11, 2021. "Frequently Asked Questions About 401(k) Plan Research" https://www.ici.org/faqs/faq/401k/faqs_401k#:~:text=In%202020%2C%20there%20were%20about,of%20former%20employees%20and%20retire es.

a pension, you gain a better understanding for what your retirement income looks like. You have the certainties of income for life.

Without a pension, you have to manage your different retirement buckets of money efficiently, provide your own pension-like stream of income, and plan appropriately to make sure that your income will last. The last thing you want to do is start the journey on the backside of life and have your income run out before you do.

If there is anything to learn from this paradigm shift, it's that you must look out for yourself. Whether you have worked for a company for two years or twenty, you are still the one who has to look out for your own best interests. That holds doubly true when it comes to preparing for retirement. If you are one of the lucky ones who still has a pension, good for you. But for the rest of us, it is likely a 401(k)—or possibly one of its nonprofit- or government-sector counterparts, a 403(b) or 457 plan—is one of your biggest assets for retirement.

Some employers offer incentives to contribute to their company plans, like a company match. On that subject, I have one thing to say: *Do it!* Nothing in life is free, as they say, but a company match on your retirement funds is about as close to free money as it gets. If you can make the minimum to qualify for your company's match at all, go for it.

Now, it's likely, during our working years, we mostly "set and forget" our 401(k) funding. Because it is tax-advantaged, your employer is taking money from your paycheck—before taxes—and putting it into your plan for you. Maybe you got to pick a selection of investments, or maybe your company only offers one choice of investment in your 401(k). Either way, while you are gainfully employed, your most impactful decision may just be the decision to continue funding your plan in the first place. But, when you are ready to retire or move jobs, you have choices to make requiring a little more thought and care.

When you are ready to part ways with your job, you have a few options:

- Leave the money where it is

- Take the cash (and pay income taxes and perhaps a 10 percent additional federal tax if you are younger than age fifty-nine-and-one-half)
- Transfer the money to another employer plan (if the new plan allows)
- Roll the money over into a self-directed IRA

Now, these are just general options. You will have to decide, hopefully with the help of a financial professional, what's right for you. For instance, 401(k)s are typically pretty closely tied to the companies offering them, so when changing jobs, it may not always be possible to transfer a 401(k) to another 401(k). Leaving the money where it is may also be out of the question—some companies have direct cash payout or rollover policies once someone is no longer employed.

Also, remember what we mentioned earlier about how we change jobs more often these days? That means you likely have a 401(k) with your current company, but you may also have a string of retirement accounts trailing you from other jobs.

I remember engaging with a client who was planning to retire in one year and wanted to make sure they had a solid game plan and the necessary income needed for their retirement budget. Each spouse had worked very hard over the years and had changed jobs several times. After an in-depth review and analysis of all of their future income sources, they were surprised to see the total of all the different retirement accounts they had from all the different employers.

They had never been counseled about the need to aggregate their different retirement accounts. They had never been told that they can move their different retirement accounts to individual retirement accounts. They thought if they moved them, they would have a taxable event.

Also, by leaving their retirement funds in each employer's retirement plan, they limited themselves to the solutions provided by only that plan. When you have your retirement assets in an individual retirement account, you have the full spectrum of financial solutions available, which can potentially provide individual solutions with guaranteed income and the ability to properly balance risk in a more diverse choice of financial options.

When it comes to your retirement income, it's important to be able to pull together *all* your assets, so you can examine what you have and where, and then decide what you will do with it.

Tax-Qualified, Tax-Preferred, Tax-Deferred ... Still TAXED

Financial media often cite IRAs and 401(k)s for their tax benefits. After all, with traditional plans, you put your money in, pre-tax, and it hopefully grows for years, even decades, untaxed. That's why these accounts are called "tax-qualified" or "tax-deferred" assets. They aren't *tax-free!* Rarely does Uncle Sam allow business to continue without receiving his piece of the pie, and your retirement assets are no different. If you didn't pay taxes on the front end, you will pay taxes on the money you withdraw from these accounts in retirement. Don't get me wrong: This isn't an inherently good or bad thing; it's just the way it is. It's important to understand, though, for the sake of planning ahead.

In retirement, many people assume they will be in a lower tax bracket. Are you planning to pare down your lifestyle in retirement? Perhaps you are, and perhaps you will have substantially less income in retirement. But many of my clients tell me they want to live life more or less the same as they always have. The money they would previously have spent on business attire or gas for their commute they now want to spend on hobbies and grandchildren. That's all fine, and for many of them, it is doable, but does it put them in a lower tax bracket? Probably not.

Keep in mind, IRAs, 401(k)s, and their alternatives have a few limitations because of their special tax status. For one thing, the IRS sets limits on your contributions to these retirement accounts. If you are contributing to a 401(k) or an equivalent nonprofit or government plan, your annual contribution limit is $20,500 (as of 2022). If you are fifty or older, the IRS allows additional contributions, called "catch-up contributions," of up to $6,500 on top of the regular limit of $20,500.[46] For an IRA, the limit is $7,000, with a catch-up limit of an additional $1,000.[47]

Because their tax advantages come from their intended use as retirement income, withdrawing funds from these accounts before you turn fifty-nine-and-one-half can carry stiff penalties. In addition to fees your investment management company might charge, you will have to pay income tax *and* a 10 percent federal tax penalty, with few exceptions.

The fifty-nine-and-one-half rule for retirement accounts is incredibly important to remember, especially when you're young. Younger workers are often tempted to cash out an IRA from a previous employer and then are surprised to find their checks missing 20 percent of the account value to income taxes, penalty taxes, and account fees.

Many millennials I see in my practice say, while they may be socking money away in their workplace retirement plan, it is often the *only* place they are saving. This could be problematic later because of the fifty-nine-and-one-half rule; what if you have an emergency? It is important to fund your retirement, but you need to have some liquid assets handy as emergency funds. This can help you avoid breaking into your retirement accounts and incurring taxes and penalties because of the fifty-nine-and-one-half rule.

---

[46] Jackie Stewart. Kiplinger.com. Dec. 17, 2021. "401(k) Contribution Limits for 2022" https://www.kiplinger.com/retirement/retirement-plans/401ks/603949/401k-contribution-limits-for-2022
[47] Fidelity.com. 2021. "IRA contribution limits." https://www.fidelity.com/retirement-ira/contribution-limits-deadlines

RMDs

Remember how we talked about the 401(k) or IRA being a "tax wrapper" for your funds? Well, eventually, Uncle Sam will want a bite of that candy bar. So, when you turn seventy-two, the government requires you withdraw a portion of your account, which the IRS calculates based on the size of your account and your estimated lifespan. This required minimum distribution, or RMD, is the government's insurance it will collect some taxes, at some point, from your earnings. Because you didn't pay taxes on the front end, you will now pay income taxes on whatever you withdraw, including your RMDs. Also, let me just remind you not to play chicken with the U.S. government; if you don't take your RMDs starting at seventy-two, you will have to write a check to the IRS for *50 percent* of the amount of your missed RMDs. With the change in law from the SECURE Act of 2019, even after you begin RMDs, you can still also continue contributing to your 401(k) or IRAs if you are still employed, which can affect the whole discussion on RMDs and possible tax considerations.

If you don't need income from your retirement accounts, RMDs can seem like more of a tax burden than an income boon. While some people prefer to reinvest their RMDs, this comes with the possibility of additional taxation: You'll pay income taxes on your RMDs and then capital gains taxes on the growth of your investments. If you are legacy minded, there are other ways to use RMDs, many of which have tax benefits.

Permanent Life Insurance
One way to turn those pesky RMDs into a legacy is through permanent life insurance. Assuming you need the death benefit coverage and can qualify for it medically, if properly structured, these products can pass on a sizeable death benefit to your beneficiaries, tax-free, as part of your general legacy plan.

ILIT

Another way to use RMDs toward your legacy is to work with an estate planning attorney to create an irrevocable life insurance trust (ILIT). This is basically a permanent life insurance policy placed within a trust. Because the trust is irrevocable, you would relinquish control of it, but, unlike with just a permanent life insurance policy, your death benefit won't count toward your taxable estate.

Annuities

Because annuities can be tax-deferred, using all or a portion of your RMDs to fund an annuity contract can be one way to further delay taxation while guaranteeing your income payments (either to you or your loved ones) later. (Assuming you don't need the RMD income during your retirement.)

Qualified Charitable Distributions

If you are charity-minded, you may use your RMDs toward a charitable organization instead of using them for income. You must do this directly from your retirement account (you can't take the RMD check and *then* pay the charity) for your withdrawals to be qualified charitable distributions (QCDs), but this is one way of realizing some of the benefits of a charitable legacy during your own lifetime. You will not need to pay taxes on your QCDs, and they won't count toward your annual charitable tax deduction limit, plus you'll be able to see how the organization you are supporting uses your donations. You should consult a financial professional on how to correctly make a QCD, particularly since the SECURE Act has implemented a few regulations on this point.[48]

---

[48] Bob Carlson. Forbes. January 28, 2020. "More Questions And Answers About The SECURE Act."
https://www.forbes.com/sites/bobcarlson/2020/01/28/more-questions-and-answers-about-the-secure-act/#113d49564869

Roth IRA

Since the Taxpayer Relief Act of 1997, there has been a different kind of retirement account, or "tax wrapper," available to the public: the Roth. Roth IRAs and Roth 401(k)s each differ from their traditional counterparts in one big way: You pay your taxes on the front end. This means, once your post-tax money is in the Roth account, as long as you follow the rules and limitations of that account, your distributions are truly tax-free. You won't pay income tax when you take withdrawals, so, in turn, you don't have to worry about RMDs. However, Roth accounts have the same limitations as traditional 401(k)s and IRAs when it comes to withdrawing money before age fifty-nine-and-one-half, with the added stipulation that the account must have been open for at least five years in order for the account holder to make withdrawals.

A Roth IRA conversion can be a great way to move taxable dollars to tax-free dollars. If you have traditional 401(k)s or IRAs, you can convert those pre-tax vehicles into a Roth IRA. This can be done in a lump sum or in bite-size pieces over several years depending on your individual tax situation. A Roth conversion is a great opportunity for future tax diversification but is not for everybody. You have to know where your break-even point is in years. We use a computer software tool that will identify each individual's break-even point and will provide valuable information that helps the decision process.

Taking Charge

As mentioned earlier, the 401(k) and IRA have largely replaced pensions, but they aren't an equal trade.

Pensions are employer-funded; the money feeding into them is money that wouldn't ever show up on your pay stub. Because 401(k)s are self-funded, you must actively and consciously save. This distinction has made a difference when it comes to funding retirement. The average 401(k) balance for a person age sixty to sixty-nine is $198,600, but the median likely tells the full story. The median 401(k) balance for a person age sixty to sixty-nine is $62,000. A general suggestion derived from those statistics is to aim, by age thirty, to have saved an amount equal to 50 to 100 percent of your annual salary.[49] For some thirty-year-olds, saving half an annual salary by age thirty is more than some sixty-to-sixty-nine-year-olds have saved for their entire lives.

There can be many reasons why people underfund their retirement plans, like being overwhelmed by the investment choices or taking withdrawals from IRAs when they leave an employer, but the reason at the top of the list is this: People simply aren't participating to begin with.

So, whether you use a 401(k) with an employer or an IRA alternative with a private company, separate from your workplace, the most important retirement savings decision you can make is to sock away your money somewhere in the first place.

---

49 Arielle O'Shea. Nerd Wallet. March 17, 2021. "The Average 401(k) Balance by Age." https://www.nerdwallet.com/article/investing/the-average-401k-balance-by-age

CHAPTER 7

Annuities

In my practice, I offer my clients a variety of products—from securities to insurance—all designed to help them reach their financial goals. You may be wondering: Why single out a single product in this book?

Well, while most of my clients have a pretty good understanding of business and finance, I sometimes find those who have the impression there must be magic involved. Some people assume there is a magic finance wand we can wave to change years' worth of savings into a strategy for retirement income. But it's not as easy as a goose laying golden eggs or the Fairy Godmother turning a pumpkin into a coach!

Finances aren't magic; it takes lots of hard work and, typically, several financial products and strategies to pull together a complete retirement plan. Of all the financial products I work with, it seems people find none more mysterious than annuities. And, if I may say, even some of those who recognize the word "annuity" have a limited understanding of the product. So, in the interest of demystifying annuities, let me tell you a little about what an annuity is.

In general, insurance is a financial hedge against risk. Car owners buy auto insurance to protect their finances in case they injure someone or someone injures them. Homeowners have house insurance to protect their finances in case of a fire, flood, or another disaster. People have life insurance to protect their finances in case of untimely death. Almost juxtaposed to life insurance, people have annuities in case of a long life; annuities can give you financial protection by providing consistent and reliable income payments.

The basic premise of an annuity is you, the annuitant, pay an insurance company some amount in exchange for their contractual guarantee they will pay you income for a certain time period. How that company pays you, for how long, and how much they offer are all determined by the annuity contract you enter into with the insurance company.

How You Get Paid

There are two ways for an annuity contract to provide income: The first is through what is called annuitization, and the second is through the use of income riders. We'll get into income riders in a bit, but let's talk about annuitization. That nice, long word is, in my opinion, one reason annuities have a reputation for mystery and misinformation.

Annuitization

When someone "annuitizes" a contract, it is the point where he or she turns on the income stream. Once a contract has been annuitized, there is no going back. With annuities, if the policyholder lives longer than the insurance company planned, the insurance company is still obligated to pay him or her, even if the payments end up being way more than the contract's actual value. If, however, the policyholder dies an untimely death, depending on the contract type, the insurance company may keep anything left of the money that funded the annuity—nothing would be paid out to the contract holder's survivors. You see where that could make some people balk? Now, modern annuities rarely rely on annuitization for the income portion of the contract, and instead have so many bells and whistles that the old concept of annuitization seems outdated, but because this is still an option, it's important to at least understand the basic concept.

Riders

Speaking of bells and whistles, let's talk about riders. Modern annuities have a lot of different options these days, many in the form of riders you can add to your contract for a fee—usually about 1 percent of the contract value per year. Each rider has its particulars, and the types of riders available will vary by the type of annuity contract purchased, but I'll just briefly outline some of these little extras:

- Lifetime income rider: Contract guarantees you an enhanced income for life
- Death benefit rider: Contract pays an enhanced death benefit to your beneficiaries even if you have annuitized
- Return of premium rider: Guarantees you (or your beneficiaries) will at least receive back the premium value of the annuity
- Long-term care rider: Provides a certain amount, sometimes as much as twice the principal value of the contract, to help pay for long-term care if the contract holder is moved to a nursing home or assisted living situation

This isn't an extensive look, and usually the riders have fancier names based on the issuing company, like "Lorem Ipsum Insurance Company Income Preferred Bonus Fixed Index Annuity rider," but I just wanted to show you what some of the general options are in layperson's terms.

Types of Annuities

Annuities break down into four basic types: immediate, variable, fixed, and fixed index.

Immediate

Immediate annuities primarily rely on annuitization to provide income—you give the insurance company a lump sum up front, and your payments begin immediately. Once you begin receiving income payments, the transaction is irreversible, and you no longer have access to your money in a lump sum. When you die, any remaining contract value is typically forfeited to the insurance company.

All other annuity contract types are "deferred" contracts, meaning you fund your policy as a lump sum or over a period of years and you give it the opportunity to grow over time—sometimes years, sometimes decades.

Variable

A variable annuity is an insurance contract with investment sub-accounts. It's sold by insurance companies, but only through someone who is registered to sell investment products. With a variable annuity contract, the insurance company invests your premiums in subaccounts that are tied to the stock market. This makes it a bit different from the other annuity contract types because it is the only contract where your money is subject to losses because of market declines. Your contract value has a greater opportunity to grow, but it also stands to lose. Additionally, your contract's value will be subject to the underlying investment's fees and limitations—including capital gains taxes, management fees, etc. Once it is time for you to receive income from the contract, the insurance company will pay you a certain income, locked in at whatever your contract's value was.

As for variable annuities, we find many times that the fees and internal expenses can be very expensive. If you experience market gains, your gains are reduced by the fees and expenses. If there are market corrections, your losses can become accelerated because fees are typically a constant in variable annuities.

I am not a big fan of variable annuities for these reasons, though I would be remiss not to point out that variable annuities have the potential for higher returns than any other type of annuity. In addition, you can purchase optional riders for added protection.

In general, variable annuities tend to be more appropriate for younger investors who have the time and risk appetite to sustain potential losses in exchange for the opportunity for higher returns.

Fixed

A traditional fixed annuity is pretty straightforward. You purchase a contract with a guaranteed interest rate and, when you are ready, the insurance company will make regular income payments to you at whatever payout rate your contract guarantees. Those payments will continue for the rest of your life and, if you choose, for the remainder of your spouse's life.

Fixed annuities don't have much in the way of upside potential, but many people like them for their guarantees (after all, if your Aunt May lives to be ninety-five, knowing she has a paycheck later in life can be her mental and financial safety net), as well as for their predictability. Unlike variable annuities, which are subject to market risk and might be up one year and down the next, you can easily calculate the value of your fixed annuity over your lifetime.

Fixed Index

To recap, variable annuities take on more risk to offer more possibilities to grow. Fixed annuities have less potential growth, but they protect your principal. In the last couple of decades, many insurance companies have retooled their product line to offer fixed index annuities, which are sort of midway between variable and fixed annuities on that risk/reward spectrum. Fixed index annuities offer greater growth potential than traditional fixed annuities but less than variable annuities. Like traditional fixed annuities, however, fixed index annuities are protected from downside market losses.

Fixed index annuities earn interest that is tied to the market, meaning that, instead of your contract value growing at a set interest rate like a traditional fixed annuity, it has the potential to grow within a range. Your contract's value is credited interest based on the performance of an external market index like the S&P 500 while never being invested in the market itself. You can't invest in the S&P 500 directly, but each year, your annuity as the potential to earn interest based on the chosen index's performance, submit to limits set by the company such as caps, spreads and participation rates. For instance, if your contract caps your interest at 5 percent, then in a year that the S&P 500 gains 3 percent, your annuity value increases 3 percent. If the S&P 500 gains 35 percent, your annuity value gets a 5 percent interest bump. But since your money isn't actually invested in the market with a fixed index annuity, if the market nosedives (such as happened during 2000, 2008 and 2020, anyone?) you won't see any increase in your contract value. Conversely, there will also be no decrease in your contract value—no matter how badly the market performed, as long as you follow the terms of the contract, you won't lose any of the interest you were credited in previous years.

So, what if the S&P 500 shows a market loss of 30 percent? Your contract value isn't going anywhere (unless you purchased an optional rider—this charge will still come out of your annuity value each year). For those who are more interested in protection than growth potential, fixed index annuities can be an attractive option because, when the stock market has a long period of positive performance, a fixed index annuity can enjoy conservative growth. And, during stretches where the stock market is erratic and stock values across the board take significant losses? Fixed index annuities won't lose anything due to the stock market volatility.

In our firm we often recommend FIAs to provide a level of protection to the portfolio first because they have no downside risk and have an opportunity for a reasonable growth. This can be especially true in a low-interest rate environment considering the adverse effect rising interest rates can have on bonds.

FIAs also contain potential income solutions that can provide a guaranteed lifetime income. You can actually build your own income stream that is guaranteed to last as long or perhaps even longer than you do. If something happens to you, your beneficiaries can receive the funds remaining in your FIA.

Other Things to Know About Annuities

We just talked about the four kinds of annuity contracts available, but all of them have some commonalities as annuities.

For all annuities, the contractual guarantees are only as strong as the insurance company that sells the product, which makes it important to thoroughly check the credit ratings of any company whose products you are considering.

Annuities are tax-deferred, meaning you don't have to pay taxes on interest earnings each year as the contract value grows. Instead, you will pay ordinary income taxes on your withdrawals. These are meant to be long-term products, so, like other tax-deferred or tax-advantaged products, if you begin taking withdrawals from your contract before age fifty-nine-and-one-half, you may also have to pay a 10 percent federal tax penalty. Also, while annuities are generally considered illiquid, most contracts allow you to withdraw up to 10 percent of your contract value every year. Withdraw any more, however, and you could incur additional surrender penalties.

Keep in mind, your withdrawals will deplete the accumulated cash value, death benefit, and, possibly, the rider values of your contract.

Annuities can be a great tool to use to provide protection in a portfolio. For clients who don't necessarily like the risk and volatility associated with the stock market, we might recommend fixed indexed annuities to provide protection and an opportunity to earn a competitive interest rate.

Annuities aren't for everyone, but it's important to understand them before saying "yea" or "nay" on whether they fit into your plan; otherwise, you're not operating with complete information, wouldn't you agree? Regardless, you should talk to a financial professional who can help you understand annuities, help you dissect your particular financial needs, and help show you whether an annuity is appropriate for your retirement income plan.

CHAPTER 8
Estate & Legacy

In my practice, I devote a significant portion of my time to matters of estates. That doesn't mean drawing up wills or trusts or putting together powers of attorney or anything like that. After all, I'm not an estate planning attorney. But I am a financial professional, and what part of the "estate" isn't affected by money matters?

I've included this chapter because I have seen many people do estate planning wrong. Clients, or clients' families, have come in after experiencing a death in the family and have found themselves in the middle of probate, high taxes, or a discovery of something unforeseen (often long-term care) draining the estate.

I have also seen people do estate planning right: clients or families who visit my office to talk about legacies and how to make them last and adult children who have room to grieve without an added burden of unintended costs, without stress from a family ruptured because of inadequate planning.

I'll share some of these stories here. However, I'm not going to give you specific advice, since everyone's situation is unique. I only want to give you some things to think about and to underscore the importance of planning ahead.

At our firm, we think it is imperative to make sure that the legal aspect of your plan is in place. We want to make sure that all of our clients have an opportunity to visit with an estate planning attorney and discuss their own personal situations.

We have strategic relationships with attorneys who will give our clients a free analysis to identify if things look okay with their current documents or if adjustments appear warranted.

You Can't Take It With You

When it comes to legacy and estate planning, the most important thing is to *do it*. I have heard people from clients to celebrities (rap artist Snoop Dogg comes to mind) say they aren't interested in what happens to their assets when they die because they'll be dead. That's certainly one way to look at it. But I think that's a very selfish way to go about things—we all have people and causes we care about, and those who care about us. Even if the people we love don't *need* what we leave behind, they can still be fined or legally tied up in the probate process or burial costs if we don't plan for those. And that's not even considering what happens if you become incapacitated at some point while you are still alive. Having a plan in place can greatly reduce the stress of those responsibilities on your loved ones; it's just a loving thing to do.

Documents

There are a few documents that lay the groundwork of legacy planning. You've probably heard of all or most of them, but I'd like to review what they are and how people commonly use them. These are all things you should talk about with an estate planning attorney to establish your legacy.

Powers of Attorney

A power of attorney, or POA, is a document giving someone the authority to act on your behalf and in your best interests. These come in handy in situations where you cannot be present (think a vacation where you get stuck in Canada) or, for durable powers of attorney, even when you are incapacitated (think in a coma or coping with dementia).

It is important to have powers of attorney in place and to appoint someone you trust to act on your behalf in these matters. Have you ever heard of someone who was incapacitated after a car accident, whether from head trauma or being in a coma for weeks—sometimes months? Do you think their bills stopped coming due during that time? I like my phone company and my bank, but neither one is about to put a moratorium on sending me bills, particularly not for an extended or interminable period. A power of attorney would have the authority to pay your mortgage or cancel your cable while you are unable.

You can have multiple POAs and require them to act jointly.

What this looks like: Do you think two heads are better than one? One man, Chris, significantly relied on his two sons' opinions for both his business and personal matters. He appointed both sons as joint POA, requiring both their signoffs for his medical and financial matters.

You can have multiple POAs who can act independently.

What this looks like: Irene had three children with whom she routinely stayed. They lived in different areas of the country, which she thought was an advantage; one month she might be hiking out West, the next she could enjoy the newest off-Broadway production, and the next she could soak up some Southern sun. She named her three children as independently authorized POAs, so, if something happened, no matter where she was, the child closest could step in to act on her behalf.

You can have POAs who have different responsibilities.

What this looks like: Although Luke's friend Claire, a nurse, was his go-to and POA for health-related issues, financial matters usually made her nervous, so he appointed his good neighbor, Matt, as his POA in all of his financial and legal matters.

In addition to POAs, it may be helpful to have an advanced medical directive. This is a document where you have pre-decided what choices you would make about different health scenarios. An advanced medical directive can help ease the burden for your medical POA and loved ones, particularly when it comes to end-of-life care.

At the end of the day, you want your legal documents to do what you want them to do! I had a client named Edna who had listed her son and daughter as power of attorney for her medical and financial affairs. Due to difficult family dynamics she had made a decision to make a change on her beneficiary designation on one of her accounts.

With her failing health, she just had her power of attorney go ahead and request the change and sign the documents with her financial institution. Edna did not know that her power of attorney document was only valid if she became totally incapacitated, which she was not. To make a long story short, the financial institution had rejected her beneficiary change request and had sent the rejection letter to her old address. The letter was never received by her or her power of attorney.

Edna passed away about six months after that and only then did the family figure out that there had been a problem and the beneficiaries had never been changed as per her request. Because she was not incapacitated at the time the request was processed and signed by her power of attorney, the change was never made. The devil is in the details!! Check your documents and beneficiary designations. Don't wait to figure this out after it is too late.

Wills

Perhaps the most basic document of legacy planning, a will is a legal document wherein you outline your wishes for your estate. When it comes to your estate after your death, having a will is the foundation of your legacy. Without one, your loved ones are left behind, guessing what you would have wanted, and the court will likely split your assets according to the state's defaults. Maybe that's exactly what you wanted, as far as anyone knows, right? Because even if you told your nephew he could have your car he's been driving, if it's not in writing, it still might go to the brother, sister, son, or daughter to whom you aren't speaking.

However, it may not be enough just to have a will. Even with a will, your assets will be subject to probate. Probate is what we call the state's process for determining a will's validity. A judge will go through your will to question if it conflicts with state law, if it is the most up-to-date document, if you were mentally competent at the time it was in order, etc. For some, this is a quick, easily-resolved process. For others, particularly if someone steps forward to contest the will, it may take years to settle, all the while subjecting the assets to court costs and attorney's fees.

One other undesirable piece of the probate process is that it is a public process. That means anyone can go to the courthouse, ask for copies of the case, and discover your assets. They can also see who is slated to receive what and who is disputing.

It's also important to remember beneficiary lines trump wills. So, that large life insurance policy? What if, when you bought it fifteen years ago, you wrote your ex-husband's name on the beneficiary line? Even if you stipulate otherwise in your will, the company that holds your policy will pay out to your ex-spouse. Or, how about the thousands of dollars in your IRA you dedicated to the children thirty years ago, but one of your children was killed in a car accident, leaving his wife and two toddlers behind? That IRA is going to transfer to your remaining children, with nothing for your daughter-in-law and grandchildren.

That may paint a grim portrait, but I can't underscore enough the importance of working with a skilled estate planning attorney to keep your will and beneficiary lines up to date as your life changes, for the sake of your loved ones.

As I mentioned above in discussing power of attorneys, we saw the importance of making sure your beneficiary designations are current and up to date. In reviewing these with folks that become our clients we find that about 40 percent of the time there are errors on their current documents.

I once worked with a client who had an issue with her deceased father's 401(k) plan. He had named her mother as primary beneficiary with no contingent beneficiaries listed. The only problem was that her mother had predeceased her father by a couple of months and the daughter was not aware of her father's old 401(k) plan until after his passing. This caused the 401(k) plan to be included in his estate, which prevented the daughter from receiving those funds as a beneficiary of the IRA. This created a much larger tax bill than she had expected.

Again, the devil is in the details! This would have been such an easy issue to correct. A stroke of the pen and it would have been fixed. Don't procrastinate!

Trusts

Another piece of legacy planning to consider is the trust.

A trust is set up through an attorney and allows a third party, or trustee, to hold your assets and determine how they will pass to your beneficiaries. Many people are skeptical of trusts because they assume trusts are only appropriate for the fabulously wealthy.

However, a simple trust will likely cost more than $1,000 if prepared by an attorney and fees can be higher for couples.[50] But a trust can help you avoid both the expense and publicity of probate, provide a more immediate transfer of wealth, avoid some taxes, and provide you greater control over your legacy.

For instance, if you want to set aside some funds for a grandchild's college education, you can make it a requirement he or she enrolls in classes before your trust will dispense any funds. Like a will, beneficiary lines will override your trust conditions, so you must still keep insurance policies and other assets up to date.

Like any financial or legal consideration, there are many options these days beyond the simple "yes or no" question of whether to have a trust. For one thing, you will need to consider if you want your trust to be revocable (you can change the terms while you are alive) or irrevocable (can't be changed; you are no longer the "owner" of the contents). A brief note here about irrevocable trusts: Although they have significant and greater tax benefits, they are still subject to a Medicaid look-back period. This means, if you transfer your assets into an irrevocable trust in an attempt to shelter them from a Medicaid spend-down, you will be ineligible for Medicaid coverage of long-term care for five years. Yet, an irrevocable trust can avoid both probate and estate taxes, and it can even protect assets from legal judgments against you.

Another thing to remember when it comes to trusts, in general, is, even if you have set up a trust, you must remember to fund it. In my thirty-nine years' work, I've had numerous clients come to me, assuming they have protected their assets with a trust. When we talk about taxes and other pieces of their legacy, it turns out they never retitled any assets or changed any paperwork on the assets they wanted in the trust. So, please

---

[50] Rickie Houston. smartasset.com. "How Much Does It Cost to Set Up a Trust? https://smartasset.com/estate-planning/how-much-does-it-cost-to-set-up-a-trust

remember, a trust is just a bunch of fancy legal papers if you haven't followed through on retitling your assets.

Again, I find that many of the trusts that folks have paid thousands of dollars for to have the document delivered in a big pleather-looking binder have never been funded. The clients were under the impression that the legal firm that put all this together for them would have taken care of the most important part of the process. This can be an unpleasant surprise.

Taxes

Although charitable contributions, trusts, and other tax-efficient strategies can reduce your tax bill, it's unlikely your estate will be passed on entirely tax-free. Yet, when it comes to building a legacy that can last for generations, taxes can be one of the heaviest drains on the impact of your hard work.

For 2017, the federal estate exemption was $5.49 million per individual and $10.98 million for a married couple, with estates facing up to a 40 percent tax rate after that. In 2022, those limits increased to $12.06 million for individuals and $24.12 million for married couples, with the 40 percent top level gift and estate tax remaining the same. Currently, the new estate limits are set to increase with inflation until January 1, 2026, when they will "sunset" back to the inflation-adjusted 2017 limits.[51] And that's not taking into account the various state regulations and taxes regarding estate and inheritance transfers.

Another tax concern "frequent flyer": retirement accounts.

Your IRA or 401(k) can be a source of tax issues when you pass away. For one thing, taking funds from a sizeable account can trigger a large tax bill. However, if you leave the assets in

---

[51] Laura Sanders, Richard Rubin. The Wall Street Journal. April 8, 2021. "Estate and Gift Taxes 2020-2021: Here's What You Need to Know." https://www.wsj.com/articles/estate-and-gift-taxes-2020-2021-heres-what-you-need-to-know-11617908256

the account, there are still required minimum distributions (RMDs), which will take effect even after you die. If you pass the account to your spouse, he or she can keep taking your RMDs as is, or your spouse can retitle the account in his or her name and receive RMDs based on his or her life expectancy. Remember, if you don't take your RMDs, the IRS will take up to 50 percent of whatever your required distribution was, plus you will still have to pay income taxes whenever you withdraw that money. Thanks to the enactment of the SECURE Act, anyone who inherits your IRA, with few exceptions (your spouse, a beneficiary less than ten years younger, or a disabled adult child, to name a few), will need to empty the account within ten years of your death.[52]

Also—and this is a pretty big also—check with an attorney if you are considering putting your IRA or 401(k) in a trust. An improperly titled beneficiary form for the IRA could mean the difference of thousands of dollars in taxes. This is just one more reason to work with a financial professional, one who can strategically partner with an estate planning attorney to diligently check your decisions.

As we have all heard before, an ounce of prevention is worth a pound of cure. I can tell you the story about John, who had not planned for his family in the event of his untimely death. One day, later on in life, he was told by his physician that his days were numbered.

John was married to his first wife for over thirty years and they had three children between them. He was a hard-working mechanic and his wife worked hard raising the children. As life will do sometimes, they eventually found themselves growing apart and finally reached the point of divorce. It was not long after that when John remarried. His new wife had three sons from her first marriage. All the children from both sides were now adults and living their own lives.

---

[52] Julia Kagan. Investopedia. October 11, 2020. "Stretch IRA." https://www.investopedia.com/terms/s/stretch-ira.asp

John's second wife became suddenly ill and passed away. About a year later, John found himself in another relationship and remarried again. Through that marriage, he added even more extended family members to the picture. When he had discovered that he had become terminally ill, he knew that he had to finally get his affairs in order after all these years of procrastination.

He had asked his youngest son if he would be the executor of his estate. With the son knowing all the family dynamics that have evolved in his father's life and having a serious talk with his father about his estates, the son knew that something had to be done to carry out his father's wishes.

John wanted 99 percent of his estate to go to the children he raised from his first marriage. But due to the fact that he had created many additional extended family members through his additional marriages, a discussion ensued over the challenges of going through probate with his current legal documents.

He and his youngest son, the executor, met with a trust attorney to discuss the best ways to carry out John's wishes. It was determined that a personal family trust was his best solution for the proper disposition of his estate after his passing.

John was able to get all of his legal documents in order prior to his passing and his son had his father's estate distributed per his father's wishes in a very short time period after John's passing. Fortunately, John received a heads up as to when he faced his final days. Because of this, he prepared for the end. Unfortunately, many people are not given this opportunity to prepare properly. This is why you cannot procrastinate with this part of your life and your final wishes! There is no question you or your family will deal with your mortality. The only question is when.

CHAPTER 9

Women Retire Too

I help men, women, and families from all walks of life on their journey to and through retirement. Yet, I want to address the female demographic specifically. Why? To be perfcctly blunt, women are more likely to deal with poverty than men when they reach retirement. One report notes that of the people living in poverty in the U.S., 56 percent are women.[53]

The topics, products, and strategies I cover elsewhere in this book are meant to help address retirement concerns for men *and* women, but the dire statistic above is a reminder that much of traditional planning is geared toward men. Male careers, male lifespans, male health care. The bottom line is women's career paths often look much different than men's, so why would their retirement planning look the same?

Women often embrace different roles and values than men as workers, wives, mothers, and daughters. They are more apt to take on roles as caretakers. They often plan for events, worry about loved ones, tend to details, and think about the future. Also, they often want everything to be just right, and they want to be right themselves. It could be you've seen the following affixed to a decorative sign, refrigerator magnet, or T-shirt: "If

[53] Robin Bleiweis, Diana Boesch. Center for American Progress. August 3, 2020. "The Basic Facts About Women in Poverty." https://www.americanprogress.org/issues/women/reports/2020/08/03/488536/basic-facts-women-poverty/

I agreed with you, we'd both be wrong." The barb features a picture of a woman speaking to a man.

If these characteristics I listed about women are accurate, shouldn't they deserve special considerations from financial professionals? The case can be made, particularly since 70 percent of men in the U.S. age 65 and older happen to be married, compared to 47 percent of women in that age classification.[54] Single women don't have the opportunity to capitalize on the resource pooling and economies of scale accompanying a marriage or partnership.

Many times through the years, I have seen the situation where women have had the primary role of working inside the home rather than outside the home. Unfortunately, the job inside the home does not provide an employer-sponsored pension or retirement plan, thus creating a dependence on the husband for their support in the retirement years.

Situations can also arise in which the pensioner accepted a single-life payout generating a greater monthly income. This can create a void in income if the spouse who has the pension passes away. If that happens to be the husband, it's worth noting that women often live longer than men. Longevity planning is often most critical for women. Within our practice, I just know that about 80 percent of my widowed clients are women.

Be Informed

It's a familiar scene in many financial offices across the country: A woman comes into an appointment carrying a sack full of unopened envelopes. Often through tears, she sits across the desk from a financial professional and apologizes her way through a conversation about what financial products she owns

---

[54] Administration for Community Living. May 27, 2021. "Profile of Older Americans." https://acl.gov/aging-and-disability-in-america/data-and-research/profile-older-americans

and where her income is coming from. She is recently widowed and was sure her spouse was taking care of the finances, but now she doesn't know where all their assets are kept, and her confidence in her financial outlook has wavered after walking through funeral expenses and realizing she's down to one income.

Often, she may be financially "okay." Yet, the uncertainty can be wearying, particularly when the family is already reeling from a loss. While this scenario sometimes plays out with men, in my experience, it's more likely to be a woman in that chair across from my desk, probably, in part, because of Western traditions about money management being "a guy thing." But it doesn't have to be this way. This all-too-common scenario can be wiped away with just a little preparation.

Talk to Your Spouse/ Work with a Financial Professional

While there are many factors affecting women's financial preparation for and situation in retirement, I cannot emphasize enough that the decision to be informed, to be a part of the conversation, and to be aware of what is going on with your finances is absolutely paramount to a confident retirement. With all the couples I've seen, there is almost always an "alpha" when it comes to finances. It isn't always men—for many of my coupled clients, the wife is the alpha who keeps the books and budgets and knows where all of the family's assets are, down to the penny—yet, statistically, among baby boomers it is usually a man who runs the books. But, as time goes on, it looks like the ratio of male to female financial alphas is evening out. According to a Gallup study, women are equally as likely to take the lead on finances as men, with 37 percent of U.S. households showing women primarily paying the bills. Half of households also say decisions about savings and investments are shared equally.[55] Whether that's the way your household works or not, there isn't anything wrong with who does what.

The breakdown happens when there is a lack of communication, when no one other than the financial alpha knows how much the family has and where. In the end, it doesn't matter who handles the money; it's about all parties being informed of what's going on financially.

There are a lot of ways to open the conversation about money. One woman started a conversation with her husband, the financial alpha, by sitting down and saying, "Teach me how to be a widow." Perhaps that sounds grim, but it was to the point, and it spurred what she said was a very fruitful conversation. Couples sometimes have their first real conversation about money, assets, and their retirement income approach, in our office. The important thing about having these conversations isn't where, it's when . . . and the best "when" is as soon as possible.

A woman once commented to me that to get this conversation rolling, she asked her husband "to teach her how to be a widow." They spent a day, just one part of an otherwise dull weekend, going through everything she might need to know. They spent the better part of two decades together after that. When he died, and she was widowed, she said the "widowhood" talk had made a huge difference. She knew who to call to talk through their retirement plan and where to call for the insurance policy.

She said the fruit of the weekend exercise they engaged in some twenty years earlier couldn't have been more apparent than when she ultimately accompanied a recently widowed friend of hers to a financial appointment. Her friend was emotional the whole time, afraid she would run out of money any day. The financial professional ultimately showed the

---

55 Megan Brenan. Gallup. January 29, 2020. "Women Still Handle Main Household Tasks in U.S." https://news.gallup.com/poll/283979/women-handle-main-household-tasks.aspx

friend that she was financially in good shape, but not before the friend had already spent months worried that each check would exhaust her bank account. That's no way to live after losing a loved one. It was preventable had her deceased spouse and financial professional included her in a conversation about "widowhood."

Spouse-Specific Options

One area where it might be especially important to be on the same page between spouses is when it comes to financial products or services that have spousal options. A few that come to mind are pensions and Social Security, although life insurance and annuity policies also have the potential to affect both spouses.

With pensions, taking the worker's life-only option is somewhat attractive—after all, the monthly payment is bigger. However, you and your spouse should discuss your options. When we're talking about both of you, as opposed to just one lifespan, there is an increased likelihood at least one of you will live a long, long time. This means the monthly payout will be less, but it also ensures that, no matter which spouse outlives the other, no one will have to suffer the loss of a needed pension paycheck in his or her later retirement years.

While we covered Social Security options in a different chapter, I think some of the spousal information bears repeating. Particularly, if you worked exclusively inside the home for a significant number of years, you may want to talk about taking your Social Security benefits based on your spouse's work history. After all, Social Security is based on your thirty-five highest-earning years.

Things to remember about the spousal benefits:[56]

---

[56] Social Security Administration. "Retirement Planner: Benefits For You As A Spouse." https://www.ssa.gov/planners/retire/applying6.html

- Your benefit will be calculated as a percentage (up to 50 percent) of your spouse's earned monthly benefit at his or her full retirement age, or FRA.
- For you to begin receiving a spousal benefit, your spouse must have already filed for his or her own benefits and you must be at least sixty-two.
- You can qualify for a full half of your spouse's benefits if you wait until you reach FRA to file.
- Beginning your benefits earlier than your FRA will reduce your monthly check but waiting to file until after FRA will not increase your benefits.

For divorcees:[57]
- You may qualify for an ex-spousal benefit if . . .
    a. You were married for a decade or more
    b. *and* you are at least sixty-two
    c. *and* you have been divorced for at least two years
    d. *and* you are currently unmarried
    e. *and* your ex-spouse is sixty-two (qualifies to begin taking Social Security)
- Your ex-spouse does not need to have filed for you to file on his or her benefit.
- Similar to spousal benefits, you can qualify for up to half of your ex-spouse's benefits if you wait to file until your FRA.
- If your ex-spouse dies, you may file to receive a widow/widower benefit on his or her Social Security record as long as you are at least age sixty and fulfill all the other requirements on the preceding alphabetized list.
    a. This will not affect the benefits of your ex-spouse's current spouse

---

[57] Social Security Administration. "Retirement Planner: If You Are Divorced." https://www.ssa.gov/planners/retire/divspouse.html

For widow's (or widower's, for that matter) benefits:[58]

- You may qualify to receive as much as your deceased spouse would have received if . . .
  a. You were married for at least nine months before his or her death
  b. *or* you would qualify for a divorced spousal benefit
  c. *and* you are at least sixty
  d. *and* you did not/have not remarried before age sixty
- You may earn delayed credits on your spouse's benefit *if* your spouse hadn't already filed for benefits when he or she died.
- Other rules may apply to you if you are disabled or are caring for a deceased spouse's dependent or disabled child.

Longevity

On average, women live longer than men. Most stats put average female longevity at about two years more than men. But averages are tricky things. A more telling statistic that surfaced in 2010 U.S. Census data revealed that more than 80 percent of U.S. centenarians, those over 100, are women. That means the vast majority of the eldest elderly are women.[59] The Population Reference Bureau projects women 85 and older will compose almost 2.9 percent of the U.S. population in 2060 and outnumber girls age zero to four (2.7 percent).

---

[58] Social Security Administration. "Survivors Planner: If You Are The Worker's Widow Or Widower."
https://www.ssa.gov/planners/survivors/ifyou.html#h2
[59] U.S. Census Bureau. December 10, 2012. "2010 Census Report Shows More Than 80 Percent of Centenarians are Women."
https://www.census.gov/newsroom/releases/archives/2010_census/cb12-239.html

On one hand, this is a Brandi Chastain moment. You know, when the American soccer icon shed her jersey to celebrate a game-winning penalty kick to win the World Cup. Seriously, how fabulous are women? They tend to be meticulous, resolute, perseverant. On the other hand, the trend for women to live longer presents longstanding financial ramifications.

Although the statistic above references a two-year difference in longevity, I have worked with women who outlived their husbands by five, ten, and even twenty-five years.

I have one client, Mary, who has been on her own for over twenty years since the passing of her husband. Tom had been the primary earner in their household. Upon his passing, Mary needed coaching and teaching on the elements of the different financial world she suddenly faced. We spent many hours together getting her up to snuff on understanding the resources that she had and how to make sure that they lasted throughout the backside of life for her. She grew proficient with her finances and was able to understand and control her financial situation.

Simply Needing More Money in Retirement

Living longer in retirement means needing more money, period. Barring a huge lottery win or some crazy stock market action, the date you retire is likely the point at which you have the most money you will ever have. Not to put too grim a spin on it, but the problem with longevity is, the further you get away from that date, the further your dollars have to stretch. If you planned to live to a nice eighty-something but live to a nice one-hundred-something, that is *two decades* you will need to account for, monetarily.

To put this in perspective, let's say you like to drink coffee as an everyday splurge. Not accounting for inflation or leap years, a $2.50 cup-a-day habit is $18,250 over a two-decade span. Now, think of all the things you like to do that cost money. Add those up for twenty years of unanticipated costs. I think you'll see what I mean.

During the 2020 onset of the coronavirus pandemic, many learned to cut costs. For some, that amounted to skipping their decadent latte. For others, however, cutbacks became acute. According to data compiled by Age Wave and Edward Jones, 32 percent of Americans plan to retire later than planned because of the pandemic. Women felt a more adverse effect. The report stipulated that 41 percent of women continued to save for retirement, compared to 58 percent of men.[60]

Yet women often tend to be planners, and during prosperous times that do not include, oh, a pandemic, they participate in retirement plans at rates 5 to 14 percentage points higher than men. Less earnings, however, often reduce the amounts women can contribute to such plans.[61]

More Health Care Needs

In addition to the cost of living for a longer lifespan is the fact aging, plain and simple, means more health care, and more health care means more money. Women are survivors. They suffer from the morbidity-mortality paradox, which states women suffer more non-fatal illnesses throughout their lifetime than men, who experience fewer illnesses but higher mortality.

Women have been found to seek treatment more often when not feeling well and emphasize staying healthy when older, according to studies.[62] So survival is on the side of the woman.

---

[60] Megan Leonhardt. cnbc.com. June 16, 2021. "58% of men were able to continue saving for retirement during the pandemic—but only 41% of women were." https://www.cnbc.com/2021/06/16/why-pandemic-hit-womens-retirement-savings-more-than-mens.html

[61] Hana Polyak. cnbc.com. March 2, 2020. "With less savings and longer lifespan, women must take 4 key steps to shore up retirement." https://www.cnbc.com/2020/02/28/longer-lifespan-fueling-women-to-take-key-steps-to-shore-up-retirement.html

[62] advisory.com. July 22, 2020. "Why do women live longer than men? It's more complicated than you think." https://www.advisory.com/en/daily-briefing/2020/07/22/longevity

However, surviving things, like cancer, also means more checkups later in life.

Widowhood

Not only do women typically live longer than their same-age male counterparts, they also have the tendency to marry men older than themselves. The numbers bear this out: Women are four times more likely to outlive their spouses than men.[63]

I don't write this to scare people; rather, I think it's fundamentally important to prepare my female clients for something that may be a startling, *but very likely,* scenario. At some point, most women will have to handle their financial situations on their own. A little preparation can go a long way, and having a basic understanding of your household finances and the "who, what, where, and how much" of your family's assets is incredibly useful—it can prevent a tragic situation from being more traumatic.

In my opinion, the financial services industry sometimes underserves women in these situations. Some financial professionals tend to alienate women, even when their spouses are alive. I've heard several stories of women who sat through meeting after meeting without their financial professional ever addressing a single question to them.

In our firm, when we work with couples, we work hard to make sure our retirement income strategies work for *both* people. No matter who is the financial alpha, it's important for everyone who is affected by a retirement strategy to understand it.

I find it to be of the utmost importance for both spouses to understand their household finances and retirement gameplan. I always emphasize how crucial it is for both spouses to attend

---

[63] Jean Chatzky. thebalance.com. January 30, 2021. "How Women Can Plan for Outliving Their Husbands."
https://www.thebalance.com/retirement-plan-for-women-outliving-husbands-4139845

every client meeting and informational event. Attendance by both spouses help each of them to understand the retirement income strategies we outline. Just as we cross-train our team to provide backup for our clients in the event of a team member getting sick or having to miss work for an extended period, it is important that each spouse be cross-trained on all the operations of the home, especially in the financial arena. If you have not done this in your family, I would highly encourage you to put a plan together to get this done.

In our firm, when we work with couples, we work hard to make sure our retirement income strategies work for both people. No matter who is the financial alpha, it's important for everyone who is affected by a retirement plan to understand it.

We have also developed a preliminary step we take to help widows look at their overall financial picture. We examine methods for the household income to be sufficient in covering expenses. It is important to have a strong grasp of the household budget.

You must know exactly what you are spending your dollars on and your sources of income. You should have a budget that incorporates not only goods, services, and utilities, but other expenses that could include recreational pursuits, insurance and taxes, charitable giving, travel, family giving, and health care costs. You want to have enough in your budget to continue to enjoy your retirement.

Taxes

One of the often-unexpected aspects of widowhood is the tax bill. Many women continue similar lifestyles to the ones they shared with their spouses. This, in turn, means continuing to have a similar need for income. However, after the death of a spouse, their taxes will be calculated based on a single filer's income table, which is much less forgiving than the couple's tax rates. With proper planning, your financial professional and tax advisor may be able to help you take the sting out of your new tax status.

Caregiving

Of the 53 million caregivers providing unpaid, informal care for older adults, 61 percent are women. Among today's family caregivers, 61 percent work and 45 percent report some kind of financial impact from providing a loved one care and support.[64] In addition to the financial burden created by caregiving responsibilities, women devote an average of forty hours each week to unpaid work when adding duties such as housekeeping.[65] So then, when can women find the time to focus long and hard on financial matters?

Unfortunately, the impact and hardships created by traditional roles for women typically do not account for Social Security benefit losses or the losses of health care benefits and retirement savings. This also doesn't account for maternity care, mothers who homeschool, or women who leave the workforce to care for their children in any way.

I don't repeat these statistics to scare you. Estimates typically place the monetary value of unofficial caregiving services across the United States at around $150 billion or more. Yet, I think the emotional value of the care many women provide their elderly relatives or neighbors cannot be quantified. So, to be clear, this shouldn't be taken as a "why not to provide caregiving" spiel. Instead, it should be seen as a call for "why to *prepare* for caregiving" or "how to lessen the financial and emotional burden of caregiving."

---

[64] caregiving.org. 2020 Report. "Caregiving in the U.S. 2020."
https://www.caregiving.org/caregiving-in-the-us-2020/
[65] Drew Weisholtz. Today. January 22, 2020. "Women do 2 more hours of housework daily than men, study says."
https://www.today.com/news/women-do-2-more-hours-housework-daily-men-study-says-t172272

Funding Your Own Retirement

For these reasons, women need to be prepared to fund more of their own retirements. There are several savings options and products, including the spousal 401(k). Unlike a traditional 401(k), where you contribute money to a plan with your employer, a spousal 401(k) is something your spouse sets up on your behalf, so he or she can contribute a portion of the paycheck to your retirement funds. This is something to consider, particularly for families where one spouse has dropped out of the workforce to care for a relative.

Also, if you find yourself in a caregiving role, talk to your employer's human resources department. Some companies have paid leave, special circumstance, or sick leave options you could qualify for, making it easier to cope and helping you stay in the workforce longer.

Saving Money

Women need more money to fund their retirements, period. But this doesn't have to be a significant burden—most of the time, women are better at saving, while usually taking less risk in their portfolios.[66] This gives me reason to believe, as women get more involved in their finances, families will continue to be better-prepared for retirement, both *his* and *hers*.

---

[66] Maurie Backman. The Motley Fool. March 4, 2021. "A Summary of 20 Years of Research and Statistics on Women in Investing." https://www.fool.com/research/women-in-investing-research/

CHAPTER 10

Indexed Universal Life Insurance

M y clients are not typically gamblers. A day at the races or the casino is more likely to give them nightmares than it is to make them eager with dollar signs in their eyes. Many would rather work with at least some guarantees than with primarily stocks and risk-based products, so, of course, that often means turning more toward life insurance, and often to a product called indexed universal life insurance, also commonly referred to as fixed indexed universal life insurance.

If you've never heard of that before, I'm not surprised. This life insurance product isn't suitable for everyone, but I want to take a second to talk about it because, for the right person, it can be a significant product in their financial arsenal.

Insurance: The Basics

If you haven't been casting around in the life insurance pond much, then let's take a second to cover the basics. During our working lives, it's likely we have some kind of basic term life policy, either privately or through our employers. Term life insurance means an individual is protected for a certain period of time—usually ten to thirty years. It typically correlates to a certain amount of wages (if it's an employer's plan) or a coverage amount chosen by the individual (if it's a person's private insurance).

At its most basic, term insurance provides funds for our loved ones and can be used for a number of purposes, including covering funeral expenses or something of that nature. Oftentimes, people will take out more than this—for instance, families with a stay-at-home parent sometimes purchase policies based on the working parent's life to cover years of income, plus the mortgage, etc. Your premium for a term life policy will be based on things like your coverage limit, your age, your health, and the term of the policy.

The older you are, the more likely it is you have health events or other issues that could make it more difficult to obtain term life insurance and the more expensive it is. Some consumers may see this as a disadvantage of term life insurance because they pay into a policy for twenty years, and then it reaches its "endowment"—the end of the contract term—and there are no additional benefits.

Permanent Insurance

Aside from the basic term life policies many wage-earners hold, insurance companies also have permanent policies, also sometimes referred to as "cash value insurance." With a permanent insurance contract, your policy will typically remain in force as long as you continue to keep it funded (there is an exception for whole life policies, which we'll get to later). A permanent insurance contract has two pieces: the death benefit and cash value accumulation.

Both are spelled out in your contract. As these products gained recognition, people began to realize the products had significant advantages when it came to taxes. I don't really want to get too technical, but it is really the technical details that make these policies valuable to their owners. That bit about tax advantages makes permanent life insurance policies attractive to consumers because, not only do they receive an income-tax-free death benefit for their beneficiaries, they may also be able to borrow against their policy, income-tax-free, if they end up needing the money.

For example, let's say Emma purchases a life insurance policy when she's thirty. She hates the idea of not having anything to show for her premiums over ten to twenty years, so she decides to use a permanent policy. Then, when she's close to fifty, her brother finds himself in dire straits. Emma wants to help, and she's been a diligent saver. The catch is most of her money is in products like her 401(k) or an annuity. These may be fabulous products suitable for her needs, but her circumstance has just changed, and she's looking for ways to help her sibling without incurring significant tax penalties.

But wait . . . she has that permanent life insurance policy! She can borrow any accumulated cash value against her policy, free of income taxes. So, let's say she borrows a few thousand dollars from her policy. She doesn't have to pay taxes on any of it. She can pay it back into her policy at any time. Then, let's say Emma dies before she "settles up" her policy (or pays back that loan). As long as she continued paying premium payments or otherwise kept her policy adequately funded until she died, then her beneficiaries will still receive a death benefit, minus the policy loan.

Are you with me so far? Here are the central themes on properly structured permanent life insurance policies: tax-free death benefit and income-tax-free withdrawals through policy loans are available as long as the premiums continue to be paid, and a minimum rate of cash value accumulation is guaranteed by the strength of the insurer.

Now, let's dive a little deeper into the two basic categories of permanent insurance on the market: whole life policies and universal life policies.

Whole Life Insurance

With whole life, an actuary in a back office has calculated what a person your age with your intended death benefit coverage, your health history, your potential lifespan—and other minutia—should pay for a premium rate. Depending on how the insurer's rate tables are calculated, your whole life policy will "endow" at a certain age—ninety, one hundred, one hundred twenty, etc.—so there is the risk you could outlive the policy, and the death benefit would pay out to you instead of your beneficiaries, which may create unplanned tax consequences.

Nonetheless, to qualify for your whole life policy, you will complete a medical questionnaire and possibly a paramedical exam, and then, based on that information, an underwriter will place you in one of these actuarial categories to determine your premium rate. One benefit of whole life insurance is the insurance company will credit a certain amount back into the policy's cash value based on your contract's guaranteed rate. Some insurance companies may also pay a dividend back to policyholders at the company's discretion.

Take Emma from the preceding example, and let's consider the scenario if her permanent insurance policy was a whole life policy. When she first purchased the contract, the insurance agent would have been able to tell her what her locked-in premium rate would be. She would pay the same amount, year after year, to keep her contract in force. And she could also calculate her policy's minimum cash value to the penny.

Universal Life Insurance

If whole life is the basic permanent life insurance policy, universal is the souped-up model. It has eight speeds, comes in many different colors, and has more options, which also means it might take some extra time and research to be thoroughly understood. But this means, if it's right for you, it can be even more customizable and fine-tuned to your specific needs.

The major differences:
- Flexible premium
- Increasing policy costs

Let's start with those increasing policy costs. Basically, the internal cost to the insurance company of maintaining your policy will increase over time, like a term insurance policy. Remember how whole life policies have those actuaries at the insurer's office calculating all of that and then determining a set rate for you to pay to cover it all? Well, with universal life, that's part of the flexible premium part. You can decide to pay a premium that will cover your future policy expenses, or you can decide to pay a premium that barely covers your current policy expenses, depending on your circumstances.

That is where these policies have gotten a bad rap in the past. If you purchase a policy and only ever pay the minimum premium required, your policy could end up losing value to the point your premium no longer covers your policy's expenses, and then the policy would lapse. That's also why it's incredibly important to work with a financial professional you trust, who can shoot straight about whether this kind of product would be appropriate for you and who makes sure you fully understand all the details.

To return to our example of Emma, though, here's how a well-set-up universal life insurance policy could work: Emma, ever the diligent saver, would have paid well over the minimum premium every month. Every time she got a raise or payroll increase, she increased the amount of premium she paid into her policy. With the policy's contractual rate of interest, she had a substantial amount of cash value accumulated in the policy. That way, when she decided to borrow money against the policy to help her brother, she could even afford to decrease her monthly payments for a time, until she was back in a better financial position.

Indexing

Now to the main event: *indexed* universal life insurance, or IUL. Like any permanent insurance, an IUL policy will remain in force as long as you continue to pay sufficient premiums, and you can borrow against your policy's cash value, income-tax-free. And, IUL policies are, at their core, universal life policies with that flexible premium. So, how are they different?

If you skim back through some of the other policy details, I covered the ability to withdraw the cash value of your policy without paying income taxes, even on the accumulation. Because of the index part of IULs, that accumulating cash value has the potential to accumulate more. An index is a tool that measures the movement of the market, like the S&P 500, or the Dow Jones Industrial Average. You can't invest directly in an index, it's just a sort of ruler.

With an IUL policy, your cash accumulation interest credits are based on an index, with what is called a "floor" and a "cap" or other limits such as a spread or participation rate. That means, if the market does well, each year your policy has the opportunity to be credited interest on the cash accumulation based on whatever your policy's index is, subject to the cap, spread, or participation rate. If the market has a bad year and the index shows negative gains, your account still gets credited, whatever your contract floor is.

So, for example, let's say your contract cap is 12.5 percent and the floor is 0 percent. If the market returns 20 percent, your contract value gets a 12.5 percent interest credit. The next year, the S&P 500 returns a negative 26 percent. The insurance company won't credit your policy anything, but you also won't see your policy value slip because of that negative performance (although policy charges and expenses will still be deducted from your policy). So, your policy won't lose value because of poor market conditions, but you can still stand to realize interest credits due to changes in an index.

Another opportunity IUL presents is for a policyholder to overfund the policy cash value in the first five or ten years and then, potentially, not have to pay any more money into the policy, letting the cash accumulation self-fund the policy. However, when overfunding an IUL policy, it is important to understand the policy may become a modified endowment contract (or MEC) if premium payments exceed certain amounts specified under the Internal Revenue Code. This can happen if a policy has been funded too quickly in its early years. For MECs, distributions during the life of the insured (including loans) are fully taxable as income to the extent there is a gain in the policy over the amount of net premiums paid. An additional 10 percent federal income tax may apply for withdrawals made before age fifty-nine-and-one-half.

So, back to our friend, Emma. If her permanent life insurance policy was an IUL, what might that have looked like? Emma saves, paying well over the mandatory minimum of her IUL policy. Let's assume the market does well for decades. Her policy accumulates a significant cash value. At some point, she stops paying as much in premium, or maybe she stops paying any premium from her own pocket at all because her policy has enough in cash value it is paying for its own expenses with the insurance company. Then, when her brother needs help, there is enough cash value stored in the policy.

It's important to note that making withdrawals or taking policy loans from a policy may have an adverse effect. You may want to talk to your financial professional to re-evaluate your premium payment schedule if you are considering this option.

If you're reeling just a bit, it's understandable. There's a lot going on with these policies. If you don't take the time to understand the basics of how they work, it's entirely possible to fall behind on premium payments and end up with a policy that lapses. Yet, if you understand the terms of your contract and are working with purpose, an IUL could be a powerful cog in the greater mechanics of your overall retirement strategy.

CHAPTER 11

Finding a Financial Professional

I was blessed to have the opportunity to enter into this industry right out of college. Karen and I had just gotten married in the summer prior to our senior years at McMurry University. We had started to begin the process of identifying our future career paths. We also knew that with marriage and a life together came the responsibility of making sure our family was protected in the event of a premature death and the need to start planning for the older person we knew we would someday become.

Reaching out to the only person I knew that could help Karen and me in this new uncharted area of our lives, I called Mr. Bishop. He took the time to drive all the way to Abilene, Texas from far east Texas just to provide guidance and direction to a newly married young couple starting the journey of life. He knew we wanted to do the best that we could to do things right.

While taking care of our business with Mr. Bishop, he asked me a simple question: "What are your plans after you and Karen graduate from college?" I told him we were not quite sure. We had begun the search process and were trying to identify our direction and find our way. He mentioned that in the business he was in, he really had an incredible opportunity to help a lot of people in ways he never could prior to his coming into this business. He loved the spirit of entrepreneurship and being able to determine his future by his work ethic and commitment. He had become very successful in the financial services industry. After careful thought and prayer, God led Karen and me into this industry, and we began the journey of becoming the masters of our new craft.

Karen and I both graduated from McMurry University with Bachelor of Business Administration degrees. I was blessed to become very involved in our local NAIFA (National Association of Insurance and Financial Advisors) organization and served at the local and state levels in Texas and New Mexico.

This is where I became the true recipient of incredible mentorship from old-school financial professionals who have impacted my professional and personal life for many years. I have become a fully registered securities representative, registered investment adviser representative, and fully licensed in property and casualty, life, health, long-term care, disability, and Medicare insurance. I obtained the LUTCF professional designation through The American College of Financial Services, which covers personal financial planning, business insurance planning, estate planning, and disability income planning. I later taught classes for all these disciplines as an instructor on behalf of The American College of Financial Services and the National Association of Insurance and Financial Advisors. I have very much embraced continuing education.

Having grown up in the country and from a small town, we learned a lot of things about life. We had to learn a wide array of skill sets, including welding, livestock husbandry, medical issues, and vehicle repair. I was also a student-athlete playing football in college. I was blessed to play the game from third grade all the way through high school and into my first two years of college. Then my luck ran out. I blew out my knee in the seventh game of my junior season at McMurry and had to have major reconstructive surgery.

Yet I was determined that my football career was not over, and I began the long, painful journey to rehabilitate my knee in time to have the opportunity to play my senior season. After lots of work, training, and commitment, I was given the green light to play. Things were going great my senior year, but seventh-game misfortune occurred once more. I got hurt again and found myself back in the hospital getting my knee worked on and put back together.

I had become such a student of my knee injury and the rehabilitation process, I felt that I could become my own doctor. However, I quickly reminded myself how much better the process would be if I relied on the help of an experienced person (my doctor) to once again guide me through the process of getting my knee back in shape. Doing so provided an opportunity for a somewhat normal active lifestyle after my second major reconstructive knee surgery.

I am continually reminded of the importance of why we should not try to be our own doctor in many areas of our life. I was told one time that true wisdom comes from completely understanding our own strengths and weaknesses, and recognizing when it's time to ask for help rather than let our pride prevent us from the blessings God has in store.

My doctor reminded me about the importance of having the right professionals throughout my recovery and rehabilitation process from knee injuries playing football. Many became involved in the process, including a physical therapist and physicians who worked to ensure that I would have the very best opportunity to live a normal active life after my second major reconstructive surgery. I knew that with all that I had learned and read, I would have a greater opportunity for success if I did not try to be my own doctor, and if I understood the medical team surrounding me had seen my situation thousands of times. That team proved more qualified to identify potential challenges, roadblocks, and possible setbacks I could encounter. I was reminded that theory is good in the classroom, but when you mix in the element called life and the unknown variables that go with it, an entire situation can change.

When we look at the overall picture of retirement today, it is much different than for previous generations. When we examine the generations of our parents and grandparents, we often find that they worked for a couple of different employers and had planned their retirement around the age of sixty-five, while likely having access to a pension and a Social Security check. In many cases, they lived five to ten years and then passed away.

Now I know that there are exceptions to this, but this is what much of those demographics looked like. In today's world, pensions are not as prevalent. A significant segment of those who make it to sixty-five are living into their eighties and a smaller, yet growing, segment lives into their nineties. We are living longer than generations in the past, and that alone puts a strain on our retirement savings to ensure that our buckets of money last longer than we do. The burden of our retirement income shifted from the employer to the employee and now we have IRAs, 401(k)s, 403(b)s, 457s, and many other qualified and non-qualified retirement accounts. Quite often now, it is an individual's responsibility to coordinate the different buckets of money and provide themselves an income that will support their own individual retirement lifestyle.

With that responsibility comes valid questions related to retirement income planning:

Do I have enough money to retire?

Am I going to outlive my money?

What if I have long-term care issues? Am I going to be ok?

What is the best way to plan for the older person I am going to someday be?

What is the best way for me to be remembered and leave a legacy?

You want to look for a financial professional who is well-rounded in all areas of financial expertise.

I suggest you look for an advisor that helps you identify any inefficiencies and will help you find solutions for your inefficiencies by constructing a financial retirement plan.

Look for an advisor that will tell you the truth about your situation and let you know if you need to right your ship and adjust your retirement income plan.

Look for an advisor that has unlimited solutions and is not limited to the philosophy and solutions of one financial institution.

A true financial professional will ask you the tough questions and serve as a coach to help organize your mix of investments, legal needs, tax-efficient strategies, and risk management are all coordinated—much like a finely tuned symphony orchestra.

You want to watch out for product salespeople that do not ask many questions and offer solutions without a thorough examination of the variables that compose your own unique situation. I see this all the time in our industry. You want to look for all the traits you would want to see in any qualified professional with whom you work.

Has the individual gone above the call of duty to improve their education and continue to study to continually grow as a competent financial advisor?

Does it appear the advisor is changing financial institutions every couple of years, or have they shown a commitment to their current financial institution?

Do they reach out and show concern for a client after a new client relationship begins?

Do they hold all the necessary licensing needed to handle clients' various needs?

Have they had numerous complaints and regulatory actions against them?

Are they active in their communities?

These are just a few things we normally look for with any professional that we entrust.

Fees

In recent years, advertising in your local newspaper has diminished. So too has the size of the paper. More people are accustomed to reading news online, or look for other sources, including those without a paywall. Advertisers don't find as much value in placing ads in the actual print version of the paper. Declines in circulation are to blame. Also, many former advertisers have company websites, which they use to drive consumer traffic.

However, if you happen to be someone who receives the newspaper in your driveway, you might have noticed that grocery store circulars are still a thing. Sure, the circulars might be a bit smaller. Yet, grocers still see some advantages to listing numerous prices for sales items in print, which readers can often scan much easier than looking up individual items on a website.

Those newspaper ads continue to be printed as a service to consumers. They want to see prices—in some cases before they ever step into the store—so they can prepare their shopping lists accordingly.

Why then should the cost of doing business with a financial professional often seem like a clandestine mystery? Well, to be blunt, it shouldn't. Consumers should know how much it will cost them to work with a financial professional and how exactly they arrive at the fees charged.

Now, fees can be troublesome. You can't get something for nothing, and fees are how many financial companies and professionals make a living. Yet, it's important to recognize even a fee of a single percentage point is money out of your pocket—money that represents not just the one-time fee of today but also represents an opportunity cost. One study found a single percentage point fee could cost a millennial close to $600,000 over forty years of saving.[67] For someone

---

[67] Dayana Yochim, Jonathan Todd. NerdWallet. "How a 1% Fee Could Cost Millennials $590,000 in Retirement Savings."

approaching retirement, how much do you think fees may have cost them over their lifetime?

It is important to look at management fees and assess if you think you're getting what you pay for. Over the course of ten years, those puppies can add up, and you may have decades ahead of you in which you will need to rely on your assets.

---

https://www.nerdwallet.com/blog/investing/millennial-retirement-fees-one-percent-half-million-savings-impact/

Acknowledgments

I have been blessed with so many mentors and relationships that have been critical to my individual growth as a person, husband, father, and leader.

First, I want to say thank you to my mother and father for instilling and teaching me the entrepreneurial spirit and commitment to hard work and service.

I want to say thank you to Bill Bishop. His mentorship and encouragement led me into this industry.

Also, thank you to Coach Terry Townzen, who taught me about commitment, discipline, character, and most of all, about the importance of having a relationship with my Lord and Savior, Jesus Christ.

And finally, to my very best friend with whom I have been blessed to experience the joy of falling in love, grow through life's ups and downs, and experience the joy of life, my incredible wife for over forty years, Karen Lyn. We have learned to laugh together, play together, cry together, pray together, and most of all live life to the fullest together. Karen has been my pillar at times of weakness and my biggest fan in times of success. Glory to God for uniting us during our college days. Thanks be to God.

About the Author

BRIAN MIRAU, MIRAU CAPITAL MANAGEMENT

As the president of Mirau Capital Management, Inc., Brian is focused on helping clients work toward their retirement dreams through well-constructed strategies for retirement income.

Brian got his start in the industry in 1983 as a financial professional who truly enjoys helping folks build, plan, and protect their financial house and plan for the other person that they will become on the backside of life.

Brian earned a BBA in finance from McMurry University. He holds his LUTCF designation from the American College of Financial Services.

On October 19, 2021, Brian was named among the Forbes 250 Financial Security Advisors in the United States.[68][69]. Brian was also named among the Forbes Top Financial Security Professionals Best-In-State list for 2022.[70] He has been published or quoted in Wall Street Select and Forbes while appearing on ABC, NBC and FOX affiliates, as well as Wall Street Select.

In his free time, Brian enjoys spending time with his family. He is very active in his cooking ministry, which has fed thousands through the years at church events, school events, Senior Olympics competitions, homeless organizations, and many community events.

Brian is a fly fisherman and enjoys hunting, golfing, backpacking, and most of all, spending time with his wife, Karen. Brian has served as the finance chair for the Grapevine Faith Christian School and Infinite Impact Ministries and remains active in both organizations. He also served as an advisor for the NFL Players Association.

---

[68] Forbes. 2022. "Top Financial Security Professional List" https://www.forbes.com/top-financial-security-professionals/#b1d5c15483f9

[69] Forbes. 2022. #247|Top Financial Security Professionals 2021: Brian Mirau" https://www.forbes.com/profile/brian-mirau/?list=financial-security-professionals/&sh=57b8b25477a8

[70] Forbes. July 28, 2022. "Top Financial Security Professionals Best-In-State" https://www.forbes.com/best-in-state-financial-security-professionals/#361c683518a8

Made in the USA
Middletown, DE
17 October 2022

12867576R00086